MetaBusiness

By
Greg Nielsen
Conscious Books
Reno, Nevada

Conscious Books
316 California Avenue, Suite 210
Reno, Nevada

First Quality Paperback Edition 1991

10 9 8 7 6 5 4 3 2 1

Library of Congress Catalog Card Number: 90-86068

ISBN 0-9619917-2-0

Printed and bound in the United States of America

Cover Illustration by Joanne Dose

Dedication

School of the Natural Order
Box 150
Baker, Nevada 89311
Write for book and tape list

Acknowledgements

Wordprocessing:	Eunice Nielsen
Cover Design:	Debra Sheehan, Shen Ink
Text Design:	Robert Bosler
Guest Chapter:	Michelle Schmidt, Chapter 8
Editing:	Linda Knudsen
Breathing Spiral	Isidore Friedman
Pumpkin Pal	Dane Nielsen

MetaBusiness

- "A MetaBusiness thrives on creativity just as much as a competitive business thrives on competition. Letting the creative forces flow freely keeps a growing MetaBusiness off the competitive levels and powerfully attuned to the creative frequencies."

- "The caretakers of a growing MetaBusiness understand to some degree the transformational power of creative energy. Welcoming and receiving an influx of creative energies means a willingness to surrender control, to feel powerless about the changes taking place, and to be fully afraid yet step forward in faith that there is a guiding intelligence behind, in, and through the process."

- "I encourage MetaBusiness leaders to create a place and a space for transformational tools to assist MetaBusiness co-creators in their personal transformations. The Energy Room would have a library of books, audio tapes, and video tapes that specifically assist individuals in their transformations."

- "MetaBusiness leaders focus on gratitude. Focusing on gratitude raises the vibration, lifting an individual out of the competitive frequencies and tuning them into the creative frequencies."

- "A MetaBusiness recognizes and acknowledges the rhythmic patterns in nature and the universe and strives to live in harmony with these natural rhythms."

- "A MetaBusiness environment where rhythmic alternation is the natural way is highly charged with creative energy. The individuals within the MetaBusiness are actually energized by being around each other."

- "A MetaBusiness leader understands the value of psychological time. If employees (co-creators) feel time dragging, why not encourage them to change that feeling? Perhaps they need a short break. Maybe they could go to the Energy Room to recharge their life force."

- "MetaBusiness co-creators know when to rest, relax, rejuvenate, regenerate, and renew. They realize that there is a dynamic balance between work time and free time. Working too much stagnates a growing business. On the other hand, playing too much leads to neglect and malnourishes the growing business."

- "Remember, when you are in a down cycle to take time to renew your purpose. Purpose is at the heart of a MetaBusiness. An unwavering purpose anchors you in the creative levels and keeps you off the competitive levels."

Introduction

Every year millions are burning out on the competitive levels. Struggle, hard work, aggression, rush, fear, lack, success, failure, greed, debt, etc.... these are the watch words of the competitive levels.

There's got to be another way. A MetaBusiness offers an alternative. A MetaBusiness creates rather than competes. By detaching mentally, emotionally, and physically from the fearful competitive frequencies you can do business on the creative levels.

A MetaBusiness creates from the "purpose motive" rather than the profit motive. Coming from purpose means feeling a heartfelt, energizing quality. You're not in it just for the money. You love what you are doing. You are energized by it.

As a MetaBusiness person you look at and handle fear, the foundation of the competitive system, in a new way. Fear is a frequency you register, you tune into, pick up on, like a radio can be tuned into a specific radio station frequency. You become more conscious the second you tune into station F-E-A-R and where you feel it is in your body.

The key to creating a MetaBusiness is self-observation. You must observe your thoughts, feelings, desires, actions, reactions, emotions, fears, etc., honestly, openly, and without judging good or bad. Simply observe, notice, become aware. Without self-observation the fearful competitive patterns will persist.

If I had to summarize this book in one word, the word would be *Gratitude*. In order for a MetaBusiness to stabilize on the creative levels, it must attune itself and resonate to *gratitude*. Regular gratitude breaks strengthen the connections to the creative levels and weaken the old ties to the competitive greed frequencies.

I advocate that a MetaBusiness create a place called the Energy Room where MetaBusiness co-creators (employers and employees) are encouraged to go to rejuvenate, renew, realign, and regenerate their life energies. I am now travelling the world assisting small, medium, and large businesses in creating an Energy Room which suits their needs.

An Energy Room would be of non-toxic construction and might include biofeedback technologies, an audio/video library, biocircuits, metaforms, color technologies, homeopathic remedies, full spectrum bulbs, crystal bowls, pyramid water, negative ion generators, magnetic massage table, octave tuning forks, etc.

Co-creator employers-employees will be encouraged to use the Energy Room whenever necessary to restore their life energies. The Energy Room is a transformational space used to assist individuals in the transition to becoming functional Energy Beings, the next step in human evolution on earth.

If you are on the competitive levels and like it, this book is not for you. Reading this book is a waste of time if you think you're going to get the competitive edge. Growing a MetaBusiness is not a fad or craze; it is an entirely different energy field requiring an evolutionary shift in consciousness.

I do not believe a competitive business is "bad" and a MetaBusiness is "good". I simply want to offer an alternative to those of us who have burned out to fearful competitive behaviors.

But if you ever find the struggle, rush, and fear tearing you apart, draining your energy, and making you sick, MetaBusiness offers another way.

With Gratitude,

Greg Nielsen, 1991

Other Books by Greg Nielsen:

Tuning to the Spiritual Frequencies

Beyond Pendulum Power

Pendulum Power

Pyramid Power

MetaBusiness Table of Contents

Chapter 1: Growing A MetaBusiness

Vision

Growing a MetaBusiness first requires a seed. The seed is vision. What is vision?

In order to clarify what vision is, let's describe what it is not. Vision is not everyday eyesight. Vision is not motivated by financial success alone. Vision is not selfish. Vision is not intellectual goal setting. Vision is not images of being first, best, or biggest.

Vision in growing a MetaBusiness has nothing to do with any of these tendencies. Most of the visions of competitive companies do include the above. A MetaBusiness vision is wider, all-inclusive, impersonal, inspired and in tune with evolutionary forces.

Vision may come in many ways. It may appear to a single individual, to a group of people who know each other, or to individuals separated by space-time who do not know each other but are connected by sympathetic vibration.

Vision may emerge through a dynamic range of experiences which may include sensory data, feelings, emotions, desires, fears, frustrations, disappointments, failures, losses, etc. In an organic way, true vision (in the MetaBusiness sense) is the seed of an evolutionary need felt first by a few, then hundreds, thousands, and millions of individuals within a cultural group.

A MetaBusiness vision is the seed of a genuine need. A competitive vision is the seed of greed. The fight-or-flight instinct is activated unconsciously. A greed seed is doomed to destruction sooner or later because it is based on conflict not cooperation.

A need seed, on the other hand, has the potential to transform individuals, the immediate community and the world. A need seed has purpose, gives clear direction and mobilizes creative forces. It is like riding the crest of a wave.

For thousands of years the greed seed vision was most dynamic when wars broke out. If you know anything about World War II you have to be amazed and astounded by the awesome mobilization of forces.

We are now coming into an era, a new age, when war is obsolete. Need seed visions will become the order of the day. MetaBusiness, in my vision, will be at the vanguard of this new age.

What kind of vision does your business operate out of? Why not create a new seed need vision out of the old vision? Let the old seeds die; let the new visions take root and live.

Structures

We are living in a time when business structures are going through major changes. There is a moving away from the "corporate ladder" structure to a variety of other structures. Growing a MetaBusiness means sensitivity to the natural formation of a business structure.

In competitive businesses, for the most part, the ladder structure is imposed upon people. The people at the top tell everyone else what to do. Those on a rung above tell others on the rung below what to do. This rigid, artificial order stimulates fear, the cornerstone of the competitive system.

A short story may illustrate my point more clearly. During the depression of the 1930's Willie worked for a ranch near Elko, Nevada. He drove a haywagon and took care of the team of horses.

One day while stacking hay on the wagon Willie drove over a slight incline. The hay was not stacked properly de-stabilizing the wagon. The wagon began to tip and turn. He jumped for his life.

As tons of hay bales began to tumble, the ranch owner (the guy at the top of the ladder) viewed the whole thing a short distance away. He rode his horse up to Willie rip-roaring mad.

He pointed his finger at Willie and yelled, "You're fired. You nearly got my best team of horses killed." He could have cared less that Willie barely escaped with his life.

Business dictatorships are beginning to die off. On a practical level business leaders are discovering that the corporate ladder structure is not very efficient, stable or profitable in the long run. A MetaBusiness' most valuable asset is the co-creator employee. And, in order for co-creator employees to be productive, happy, and committed, new business structures are being created.

A MetaBusiness leader cannot control, impose or dictate the company's structure. Instead, he or she must sense the direction in which it is forming and allow it to take shape. A natural order structure emerges in response to genuine needs, cares, understandings, loves, joys, and interests of co-creator employers/employees.

Another priority for a MetaBusiness leader is to create a work environment which is as free as possible from fear, guilt and shame. These negative emotions when out-of-control suffocate the growing MetaBusiness more than anything else. Assure and reassure the co-creator employees that fear, guilt and shame are not necessary. Encourage freedom, creativity, love, humor, joy, patience, etc.; then watch the MetaBusiness flourish on multiple levels including the spiritual and financial.

Creations

Once a need vision arises and a structure forms to contain the vision, creative energies are released. This is a powerful time in the growing of a MetaBusiness. Creative energies explode and implode with new ideas, possibilities, designs, processes, products, and services.

The creative forces are exciting, inspiring, exhilarating, stimulating, and energizing. There's a feeling in the air that "anything goes." The MetaBusiness co-creators play with different combinations and permutations. (See Chapter 17, "*The Science of Synthesis*" in *Tuning to the Spiritual Frequencies* by Greg Nielsen.)

There is a profound difference between a growing MetaBusiness and a developing competitive business when it comes to the creative phase. A competitive business tends to be fearful of creative energies because they mean change, the unknown, the unexpected, the new, the uncontrollable, etc. Creativity shakes up the status quo, the established order, and triggers the fight-or-flight mechanism in those entrenched in unconscious power kingdoms.

A MetaBusiness, on the other hand, thrives on creativity just as much as a competitive business thrives on competition. Letting the creative forces flow freely keeps a growing MetaBusiness off the competitive levels and powerfully attuned to the creative frequencies.

A competitive business tends to focus on what the competition is doing. This often leads to imitation of the competition. Creativity is squelched. The fear of being beaten out by the competition escalates.

Many fear-ridden competitive companies use lying, cheating, stealing, manipulating, coercion, etc., to get one creative idea from the apparently more successful competition. A MetaBusiness does not need to engage in such unscrupulous activities, which generate even more fear, since the creative energies generate a wealth of creative ideas.

Since creativity is the life blood of a MetaBusiness, it is wise for MetaBusiness leaders to encourage co-creator employees to pursue creative hobbies and interests in their personal lives. Whether dancing, singing, drama, painting, sculpting, or playing a musical instrument, tapping into creativity for fun, play and enjoyment will enhance the nurturing creative forces. . . the need seed vision. Creativity allows the evolving company structure to breathe with flexibility.

Transformations

During an intense creative phase the growing MetaBusiness will go through transformations. The spontaneous release of creative energies stimulates greater awareness. The co-creator employer/employee must be sensitive and flexible to the transformations.

Selfish, egotistical, prideful, greedy, etc., people will, for the most part, feel threatened, out-of-control and powerless during the transformational cycle. Refusing to be sensitive, refusing to be more conscious usually means the creative energies will be squelched. The opportunity transformation brings will be lost.

The profit motive, greed, fear, competition, the work ethic are dominating frequencies in the fight-or-flight competitive world. Once a competitive business crystallizes around these automatic, mechanical and habitual frequencies, new awareness and creativity are not allowed to transform the business structure.

The caretakers of a growing MetaBusiness understand, to some degree, the transformational power of creative energy. Welcoming and receiving an influx of creative energies, means a willingness to surrender control, to feel powerless about the changes taking place and to be fully afraid yet step forward in faith that there is a guiding intelligence behind, in and through the process.

I encourage MetaBusiness leaders to create a place and a space for transformational tools to assist MetaBusiness co-creators in their personal transformations. The Energy Room, as I call it, would have a library of books, audio tapes and video tapes which specifically assist individuals in their transformations.

Besides the library, there are energy tools like negative ion generators, relaxation circuits, alphatrons, metaforms, hemi-sync music, etc., that increase, balance and align energy. The Energy Room gives MetaBusiness co-creators a place to go when they feel unstable, drained, tired, lost, confused, fearful, scared, etc. It's common for these and other de-stabilizing feelings to surface during a creative energy cycle.

It is critical that a MetaBusiness encourage its co-creators to experience the disruptive and disturbing feelings and emotions fully and then return in a natural rhythmical cycle to peace and poise. If the process is not encouraged openly and on a practical level, as the Energy Room provides, the growing MetaBusiness may go through a crisis (which is not necessarily bad) where competitive forces are unleashed.

The maelstrom that follows may damage the MetaBusiness beyond repair or detune it temporarily from the creative levels. In either case, the transformations will usually be aborted.

Manifestations

The next step in growing a MetaBusiness is manifestations. Products, services and systems are generated which fulfill genuine needs. The quality of peoples' lives are improved. The products, services and systems created by a MetaBusiness save time, money and energy. Their customers and clients receive more in use value than they pay in cash value.

Since the manifestation of their products, services and systems are created rather than copied, they are innovative, original and truly new. A competitive business operating from a fight/flight instinctive level cannot tune into the creative frequencies. They are unconsciously attached to the fear frequencies. As a result, they copy; they do not create.

Pirating, copying an original design or creation, is a big competitive business. Watches, clothing, art, toys, etc., are copied and sold at substantially lower prices. Both the customers and the originators are ripped-off.

The fearful competitive energies dominate the global economic system. Greed, it seems, has become acceptable as perfectly all right. What is greed? Greed is an insensitive, unbalanced, sucking vortex which is insatiable. It is the fight/flight instinct gone haywire.

On a purely practical level, greed is not good for business. Greed has its own built-in self-destruct button. Greed blinds. Greed feels all-powerful. Greed takes uncalculated risks. Greed will gamble it all on an illusion. How many people have lost their life savings in scams?

A growing MetaBusiness detaches itself as much as possible from greed. It is a powerful, alluring and seductive force. You must notice it. You must acknowledge it when you're identified with it and let it go. It will promise you more, but you'll end up with less.

When you feel you want more now, in a hurry, change your attention. Focus on the limitless supply. Greed gives the illusion that the supply is limited. Focus on gratitude. Greed gives the illusion you did it all yourself. Focus on your heartfelt vision. Greed gives the illusion that renewing purpose is a waste of time and unprofitable.

Manifesting products, services and systems will generate cash flow and profits. A growing MetaBusiness must stay off the competitive/greed frequencies. Getting caught in their undertow can drown a MetaBusiness, choking off the fresh air of creative energies. Greed is not good for business.

Re-Creations

After manifesting products, services, and systems, a specific length of time passes in which a MetaBusiness' manifestations are fulfilling genuine needs on a creative level. As time passes, the customers' needs continue to change. A growing MetaBusiness remains firmly and flexibly in the creative energies by being conscious and responsive to changing needs. This sixth step in growing a MetaBusiness I call Re-Creations.

Let's review the six steps in growing a MetaBusiness:

1. Vision

2. Structures

3. Creations

4. Transformations

5. Manifestations

6. Re-Creations

The Re-Creation phase of growing a MetaBusiness is both the end and beginning of a MetaBusiness growth cycle. The on-going cycle is based on the Law of the Breathing Spiral (see figure #1 on page 1-8). On each turn of the spiral the process repeats itself in a slightly different way. After six turns of the growth spiral, a major transformation occurs.

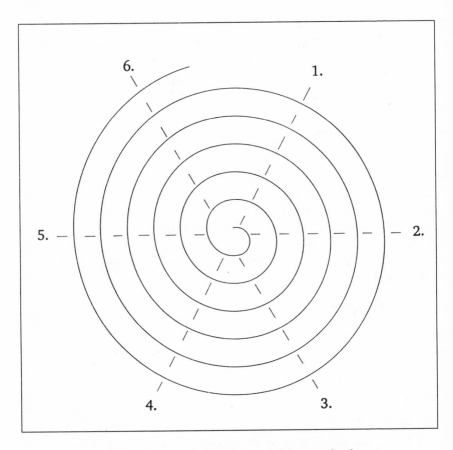

Figure 1: Law of the Breathing Spiral

In the Re-Creation stage the MetaBusiness co-creators become conscious that the customers' needs are not being adequately fulfilled. They respond in a flexible and timely way by refocusing the vision, reshaping the structures, releasing creativity, going through another transformation and manifesting new products, services and systems.

A competitive business has difficulty growing according to the Law of the Breathing Spiral. Because of the fear and greed, it get stuck in a rut. It keeps going in a circle like a dog chasing its own tail.

When a competitive business hits on a product, service or system that generates substantial profits, it tends to get stuck. It wants the good times to last forever by keeping everything the same and preserving the status quo.

As a result, it stops growing. It cannot break out of the circle into the spiral and begin growing and breathing like a MetaBusiness. The life force is cut off from the business force-field. Its breathing becomes more shallow, eventually stopping altogether. A business dies.

Summary of Chapter 1

1. A MetaBusiness vision is wider, all-inclusive, impersonal, inspired and in tune with evolutionary forces.

2. Vision may come in many ways. It may appear to a single individual, to a group of people who know each other or to individuals separated by space-time who do not know each other but are connected by sympathetic vibration.

3. A MetaBusiness vision is the seed of a genuine need. A competitive vision is the seed of greed. The fight-or-flight instinct is activated unconsciously. A greed seed is doomed to destruction sooner or later because it is based on conflict not cooperation.

4. A need seed, on the other hand, has the potential to transform individuals, the immediate community and the world. A need seed has purpose, gives clear direction and mobilizes creative forces. It is like riding the crest of a wave.

5. Growing a MetaBusiness means sensitivity to the natural formation of a business structure.

6. In a competitive business the ladder structure is imposed upon people. The people at the top tell everyone else what to do. Those on a rung above tell others on the rung below what to do. This rigid, artificial order stimulates fear, the cornerstone of the competitive system.

7. A MetaBusiness' most valuable asset is the co-creator employee. And, in order for co-creator employees to be productive, happy and committed, new business structures are being created.

8. A MetaBusiness leader cannot control, impose or dictate the company's structure. Instead, he or she must sense the direction in which it is forming and allow it to take shape. A natural order structure forms in response to genuine needs, cares, understandings, loves, joys, and interests of co-creator employer/employees.

9. Once a need vision arises and a structure forms to contain the vision, creative energies are released. This is a powerful time in the growing of a MetaBusiness. Creative energies explode and implode with new ideas, possibilities, designs, processes, products, and services.

10. A competitive business tends to be fearful of creative energies because they mean change, the unknown, the unexpected, the new, the uncontrollable, etc. Creativity shakes up the status quo, the established order, and triggers the fight-or-flight mechanism in those entrenched in unconscious power kingdoms.

11. A MetaBusiness thrives on creativity just as much as a competitive business thrives on competition. Letting the creative forces flow freely keeps a growing MetaBusiness off the competitive levels and powerfully attuned to the creative frequencies.

12. A competitive business tends to focus on what the competition is doing. This often leads to imitation of the competition. Creativity is squelched. The fear of being beat out by the competition escalates.

13. Since creativity is the life blood of a MetaBusiness, it is wise for MetaBusiness leaders to encourage co-creator employees to pursue creative hobbies and interests in their personal lives.

14. The caretakers of a growing MetaBusiness understand, to some degree the transformational power of creative energy. Welcoming and receiving an influx of creative energies means a willingness to surrender control, to feel powerless about the changes taking place and to be fully afraid yet step forward in faith that there is a guiding intelligence behind, in and through the process.

15. I encourage MetaBusiness leaders to create a place and a space for transformational tools to assist MetaBusiness co-creators in their personal transformations. The Energy Room would have a library of books, audio tapes and video tapes that specifically assist individuals in their transformations.

16. Besides the library, there are energy tools like negative ion generators, relaxation circuits, alphatrons, metaforms, hemi-sync music, etc., that increase, balance and align energy.

17. The Energy Room gives MetaBusiness co-creators a place to go when they feel unstable, drained, tired, lost, confused, fearful, scared, etc. It's common for these and other de-stabilizing feelings to surface during a creative energy cycle.

18. Since the manifestations of a growing MetaBusiness' products, services and systems are created rather than copied, they are innovative, original and truly new.

19. A competitive business operating from a fight/flight instinctive level cannot tune into the creative frequencies. They are unconsciously attached to the fear frequencies. As a result, they copy; they do not create.

20. Greed has become acceptable as perfectly all right. What is greed? Greed is an insensitive, unbalanced, sucking vortex which is insatiable. It is the fight/flight instinct gone haywire.

21. On a purely practical level, greed is not good for business. Greed has its own built-in self-destruct button. Greed blinds. Greed feels all-powerful. Greed takes uncalculated risks. Greed will gamble it all on illusion.

22. When you feel you want more now, in a hurry, change your attention. Focus on the limitless supply. Greed gives the illusion that the supply is limited. Focus on gratitude. Greed gives the illusion you did it all yourself. Greed gives the illusion that renewing purpose is a waste of time and unprofitable.

23. The six steps in growing a MetaBusiness are:
    1. Vision
    2. Structures
    3. Creations
    4. Transformations
    5. Manifestations
    6. Re-Creations

24. As time passes, the customers' needs change. A growing MetaBusiness remains firmly and flexibly in the creative energies by being conscious and responsive to changing needs. This is the Re-Creation phase.

25. The Re-Creation phase of growing a MetaBusiness is both the end and beginning of a MetaBusiness growth cycle.

26. A MetaBusiness grows according to The Law of the Breathing Spiral. On each turn of the spiral the six steps repeat in a slightly different way. After six turns in the growth spiral, a major transformation occurs.

27. A competitive business has difficulty growing according to The Law of the Breathing Spiral. Because of the fear and greed, it gets stuck in a rut. It keeps going in a circle like a dog chasing its own tail.

Chapter 2: Purpose Balanced With Profit

The Profit Motive

If a business, company or corporation is operating purely from a profit motive, it cannot survive. Yes, for a time it may show soaring profits for a few months, even years. But eventually, in an attempt to push profit above all else, the company decision makers will take risks which will jeopardize the business' very existence.

Years ago I worked for a New York area department store chain. About the time I started with their 14th Street outlet, a new management team took over. It did not take long to see what their motive was, PROFITS!

First, they stopped hiring full-time employees. Sure, hiring part-timers drastically reduced their payroll, unemployment insurance and employee benefit expenses.

True, profits increased dramatically for a time. But in the long run their short sightedness resulted in dramatic losses and the eventual closing down of the entire chain.

What happened? The profit motive, with its roots in selfishness, greed, and a "survival of the fittest" mentality began to spread like an emotional virus throughout the business.

The personnel department began to hire people who were not looking for a long-term career position but, at minimum wage, a short-term source of income. As a result, the quality of service dropped dramatically.

Customers used to seeing the same faces, for years providing knowledgeable service, suddenly were confronted with new faces who had little if any product knowledge. At a geometrically rapid rate long term customers went elsewhere.

The loyal customer base this department store chain built over 30 years disappeared and was replaced by "lowest price" motivated customers who felt little if any loyalty. Consequently, when there was a sale, the store was busy. No sale, the place was dead.

Obviously, in and of itself, there is nothing wrong with profit. Profit is a necessity for a business to survive, to grow and to prosper. The "profit only" motive in a business leads to non-survival, decay and financial losses.

If you own a business, work for a business or plan on going into a business which is solely or mostly profit motivated, you may want to reconsider. For long-term financial stability, as well as mental, emotional, physical and spiritual balance, you may want to seriously consider and introduce the "purpose motive" in your business life.

The Purpose Motive

What do you love doing more than anything else? What do you enjoy doing so much it's never work? If you know the answers to these questions, you know what the purpose motive feels like.

When you are in tune with your purpose, you feel like you're doing exactly what you're supposed to be doing. You experience a kind of inner contentment and confidence which permeates your personality. Others sense you are doing what you love.

A business that, at its heart, is filled with purpose is a MetaBusiness. No matter what the ups and downs may be financially, the purpose motive remains at the core.

What is purpose? Every person, place and thing throughout the universe and dimensions has a structure. A hammer, for example, is designed specifically to drive nails. It has a particular structure which efficiently accomplishes a particular function.

Have you ever needed a screwdriver and all you had was a hammer? You foolishly hammer the screw into the wall. You end up with a hole in the wall.

When you go against the natural order of people, places and things, when you use a hammer to drive a screw into a wall, you are not in tune with purpose. What results? Destructive (de -structuring) events occur, a hole in the wall.

If you are miserable, drained, angry, negative, etc., in your present business, profession or job, chances are you're going against your natural structure and function; you are out of tune with your purpose.

As a very wise teacher told me, "If you're a toaster, don't try to be a refrigerator. A toaster trying to make ice cubes can only lead to disappointment and frustration. If you're a toaster, make toast!"

A MetaBusiness is attuned to purpose. Its products and/or services reflect the purpose motive. The more precisely tuned a business is to purpose the better the quality of services and products.

As the products and services produced and provided by a business diminishes in quality the purpose motive has diminished proportionately. Can you recall a business where this has happened? Perhaps you have worked for such a business, maybe even owned one yourself.

For a number of years U.S. auto manufacturers suffered a sales slump. The quality of their product diminished as the quality of Japanese car makers increased. The purpose motive, you can be sure, was being replaced by the profit motive. Greed, an unbalanced desire for more, infiltrated the thinking of corporate officers and line workers alike.

Ask yourself, "How strong is the purpose motive where you work?" Do you feel purpose in the midst of your daily activities? Are you a hammer happy striking nails? Or are you miserable hammering screws?

Maybe it's about time you find your purpose. If you own or run a business purely for profit, maybe it's about time you infuse the business with vision and the purpose motive.

Finding Your Purpose

People often ask me, "How do I know when I've found my Purpose?" First of all, when someone asks that question, you know they are still in the process of attuning themselves to their purpose. When you find your purpose, there will be no doubt in your heart.

To answer the question, living from purpose is energizing, rejuvenating, creative, mentally/emotionally stimulating and spiritually uplifting. Your life feels significant, meaningful and rewarding. You feel that you are fulfilling your destiny, accomplishing your appointed task, following your heart.

Now, the next question becomes "How do you find your purpose?"

Step 1 RESOLVE TO FIND YOUR PURPOSE.

Make up your mind once and for all that nothing and no one will prevent you from finding and following your path.

There are many distractions in life. It's easy to find excuses. It's even easier to put it off until tomorrow. Make a commitment to yourself that even if you must travel to the ends of the earth you are determined to find the purpose that energizes your life.

Step 2 ASK FOR GUIDANCE.

A MetaBusiness recognizes and acknowledges the one power, one plan, one process, one presence. Call it what you want. Whatever your religion or belief system calls it, use that name if you prefer. The point is, It Is. Your purpose is part of Its purpose.

From the bottom of your heart, from the very core of your being, ask for guidance. Specifically, ask to be assisted in the process of finding and following your purpose.

Step 3 GATHER SELF-KNOWLEDGE.

Through self-observation become the world's greatest authority on yourself. Without self-criticism or over-analysis, notice your likes and dislikes, your thoughts and images, your interactions and reactions to others, etc.

As you get to know yourself better, you will become more conscious of your structure. Remember, structure leads to function and function leads to purpose.

Are you a communicator? Are you a creator? Are you a server? Are you a nourisher? What do you notice you LOVE doing when you're doing it? What you love to do points the way. Follow your heart and you have found your purpose.

Manifesting Your Purpose

In order to manifest your purpose, persistently and consistently, day in and day out, you must come from a consciousness of peace and poise. If you operate a business or work for a business that comes from unconscious anxiety, fear and greed, purpose cannot be manifested. Only more anxiety, fear and greed is manifested.

Manifesting your purpose requires regular renewal of peace and poise. This means setting aside time to relax, meditate, pray, be quiet, listen to the silence, contemplate, etc. Whatever naturally brings you to a consciousness of peace and poise, use on a regular rhythmic basis to renew your bond with the presence.

A business is a living entity. If it is a greed vacuum created simply to suck money, its' lust for profits makes it bigger and bigger until it bursts like a balloon. As a profit monster it uses and abuses people, places and things in the name of "democracy", "free enterprise", and "capitalism".

A MetaBusiness is a living entity that respects and protects the people, places and things (also living entities) it interacts with. A MetaBusiness is a living environment through which an individual or individuals can manifest their life purpose. A MetaBusiness, at its center, needs a consciousness of peace and poise in order to be receptive and sensitive to meaningful priorities.

As you make quiet time, rhythmic respites from daily routine, the contemplative mind will effortlessly tune into meaningful priorities. The head of a MetaBusiness will see what is needed, what is wisest to do next.

If you have ever or are now running a business, you know the vast number of potential decisions which are possible. Often, one foolish decision, no matter how reasonable it may appear, will threaten a business' very survival.

It makes sense then to make the wisest decisions possible in manifesting a business' purpose as well as your purpose. From an actual experience of the energies of peace and poise, meaningful priorities will emerge. You must recognize their wisdom and implement them with an acute sense of timing.

The Purpose/Profit Balance

At one time, I had dealings with a potential MetaBusiness called *Dream Songs*. They were a combination self-improvement bookstore and giftshop.

When they first opened, I visited with the owners. It was evident that purpose was abundant. They wanted to become a spiritual center, a place for meditation and peace.

Within six months, however, they closed down. What happened?

Purpose was out-of-balance with profits. Their purpose was so powerful they were blinded by idealism. They did not clearly perceive the profit process.

To be overly identified with purpose is just as out-of-balance as to be overly identified with profits.

The purpose motive must be at the center of a MetaBusiness. Then, in its day-to-day operation, profitable practices must be implemented for the purpose to manifest in quality products and/or services.

A sound business sense must be utilized. Purpose alone does not guarantee a successful business. True, a MetaBusiness' success is not measured in dollars and cents; it is measured by the inner gratification of knowing others have genuinely benefited from its goods and/or services.

Once your purpose is clear, then extensive business fact gathering is a must. Name, location, hours, overhead, cash flow, marketing, etc. Many practical decisions must be made, put into practice and continuously monitored.

A MetaBusiness makes a profit. It is self-sufficient; it supports itself.

Dream Songs purpose was not in balance with profit. Their location worked against them from the start. The population base to draw from was plainly too small. The list goes on.

In the coming years as more of us become attuned to our life purpose, we naturally want to spend our time in an harmonious work environment. If you decide to create a MetaBusiness, balance purpose and profit. Purpose is not better than profit. It gives heart to an otherwise cold, calculating and competitive capitalism.

A Common Purpose

When a group of people pull together toward a common purpose, remarkable events occur. A common purpose is a mighty force that can change the very fabric of a nation, culture, community, organization or company.

A MetaBusiness is an organization that is magnetized. Each individual in the business is more or less in tune with their life purpose. A magnet is a magnet because the atoms are aligned creating a magnetic field (see figure 2 on page 2-8). A MetaBusiness is a MetaBusiness because the individuals are aligned in a common purpose.

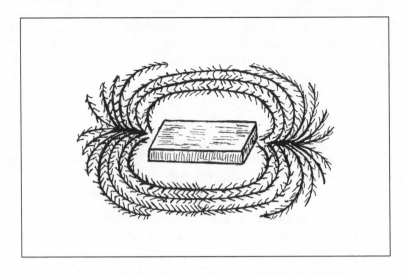

Figure 2: The Aligned Field of a Magnet

True, a profit motivated business can be magnetically aligned toward a common purpose. The difference, however, is in a MetaBusiness each person is attuning to their individual purpose as a well as to the common purpose. As a result, individual purposes merge, to some degree, with the common purpose.

Running a MetaBusiness requires extra special care in the hiring process. Mixing purpose-motivated individuals with profit-motivated people will inevitably result in explosive events.

Before you hire anyone, you must not only review their outer qualifications, but also their inner qualifications. Are they just looking for a job, or are they full of purpose and prepared to manifest their purpose even more within and through a MetaBusiness?

I have done consulting for MetaBusinesses in the area of common purpose. I recall one situation in particular where a MetaBusiness owner hired an employee who appeared to be in common purpose with the store. That's not how it turned out.

When the owner talked with me, she was very concerned because several long-term customers complained to her about this employee. Apparently the employee in question was dogmatically force feeding her belief system to the customers. In addition, she was coming off as if the business were hers. From an energy point of view, she was taking over the business.

During the time this cross-purpose employee worked at this retail business, sales dropped progressively each month. It was obvious she wanted to use the business for her personal power and selfish purposes.

The owner cut back the employee's hours as a direct result of lower sales. The next month sales increased. The profit motivated employee quit in part because she did not have enough hours. Sales increased even more.

Summary of Chapter 2

1. If a business, company or corporation is operating from a profit motive, it cannot survive.

2. For long-term financial stability, as well as mental, emotional, physical and spiritual balance, you may want to consider and introduce the "purpose motive" into your business life.

3. A business that, at its heart, is filled with purpose is a MetaBusiness. No matter what the ups and downs may be financially, the purpose motive remains at the core.

4. If you are miserable, drained, angry, negative, etc., in your present business, profession or job, chances are you're going against your natural structure and function. You are out-of-tune with your purpose.

5. A MetaBusiness' products and/or services reflect the purpose motive. The more precisely tuned a business is to purpose the better the quality of services and products.

6. Living from purpose is energizing, rejuvenating, creative, mentally/emotionally stimulating and spiritually uplifting. Your life feels significant, meaningful and rewarding. You feel like you are fulfilling your destiny, accomplishing your appointed task, following your heart.

7. How do you find your purpose?
    Step One: Resolve to find your purpose.
    Step Two: Ask for guidance.
    Step Three: Gather self-knowledge.

8. In order to manifest your purpose, persistently and consistently, day in and day out, you must come from a consciousness of peace and poise.

9. A business that is a profit monster uses and abuses people, places and things in the name of "democracy", "free enterprise", and "capitalism".

10. A MetaBusiness is a living entity that respects and protects the people, places and things (also living entities) it interacts with.

11. From your experience of the energies of peace and poise meaningful priorities emerge. You must recognize their wisdom and implement them with an acute sense of timing.

12. To be overly identified with purpose is just as out-of-balance as to be overly identified with profits.

13. A Metabusiness makes a profit. It is self-sufficient; it supports itself.

14. A MetaBusiness balances purpose and profit. Purpose gives heart to an otherwise cold, calculating and competitive profit motive.

15. A MetaBusiness is an organization that is magnetized. Each individual in the business is more or less in tune with their life purpose.

16. As a result, individual purposes merge, to some degree, with the common purpose.

17. Running a MetaBusiness requires extra special care in the hiring process. Mixing purpose motivated individuals with profit motivated people will inevitably result in explosive events.

18. Before you hire anyone, you must not only review their outer qualifications, but also their inner qualifications.

Chapter 3: Creativity Replaces Competition

Competition Conflicts, Creation Cooperates

The competitive mind-set is deeply ingrained in our political, social, economic, religious, etc., systems. The competitive spirit is considered a virtue. The most competitive people are revered with fame and rewarded with wealth.

Fortune magazine quoted a 42-year old manufacturing manager as saying, "I pride myself on being competitive. My wife and I are competitive, my kids are competitive. Competition brings out your best."

Here we have it. "My wife and I are competitive," says it all. The conflict of the sexes! Man versus woman! Who wins, who loses!

What happened to love, harmony, cooperation and creativity?

Yes, it sometimes appears that competition "brings out the best". The survival of the fittest mentality often brings out the best, but it is usually temporary. If you look at life as a whole, competition brings out the worst.

The *Fortune* article was titled "The Workaholic Generation". Later in the piece, the "successful" manufacturing manager contradicts himself (which is consistent with the competitive mind-set), "I'm a little insecure, like a number of people. My wife says that I put in so much time at work because that's where I get stroked."

The competitive life brings conflict, the "best" in one area, the "worst" in another. It brings about imbalance, disharmony, one-sidedness and addictive behavior.

A MetaBusiness rejects competitive conflict in favor of cooperative creativity.

Wallace Wattles writes in *Scientific Financial Success*:

"You must get rid of the thought of competition. You are to create, not to compete for what is already created. You are to become a creator, not a competitor. You are going to get what you want, but in such a way that when you get it every other person will have more than he has now."

(To order *Scientific Financial Success* see the back of this book).

Creation cooperates and benefits from the creative mind-set. A MetaBusiness originates, creates a service and/or product which takes nothing away from anyone, takes advantage of no one.

Creation cooperates with the natural process. In a MetaBusiness the purpose harmonizes with the purpose that is in all.

Competition is Fearful, Creation is Faithful

Old competitive fears often die hard. Situations may arise where competitive fears surface and pull you into feelings of lack. You, then, buy into the belief that the supply is limited.

Remember, just because you believe something does not mean you practice it consistently. Let's say you create a computer software system that fulfills a genuine need. Sales increase dramatically.

Before too long several other companies are producing similar software. If you identify with the thoughts, "They're taking my business away; they're stealing my customers; they're copying our products," then you connect with the fearful competitive energies.

A MetaBusiness leader renews her or his faith when competitive fears temporarily arise by recalling that there is a "limitless supply in formless substance." A knowing faith is powerfully felt in the process of creation. By communicating your thoughts to formless substance, you can cause the creation of the "things" (events / services / processes / products) thought about.

Competition is fearful; creation is faithful. A MetaBusiness has faith in the creative process and knows how to put it into action. As a MetaBusiness leader you may from time to time become temporarily identified with lack. Your fears may, for a time, blind you to the limitless supply focusing, instead, on the apparent limited supply.

When that happens, stop focusing on the visible supply. Change the focus of your attention *"placing it in knowing faith on the limitless supply in formless substance. Know that it is coming to you as fast as you can receive and use it. Nobody, by cornering the visible supply can prevent you from getting what is yours."* Wallace Wattles

Competition Takes, Creation Gives

A business that restricts, drains, frightens, punishes and generally leaves the customer/client with less life, health, happiness and love is on the competitive level. A business that releases, energizes, enlightens, frees and generally leaves the customer/client with more life, health, happiness and love is on the creative level. In short, competition takes and creation gives.

For a time I sold electronic phone systems to businesses. The product was excellent. Purchasing an office phone system saved companies thousands of dollars over renting or leasing phones from Ma Bell.

In sharp contrast to the quality product was the inadequate service provided by this private phone company. Once the phone system was installed minor adjustments were usually required. Service calls, for the most part, were practically ignored.

Needless to say, the customers felt cheated, robbed, used and taken. Many of the installers and salespeople resigned (myself included) because the owner refused to provide excellent support services.

The owner enticed potential customers with a superior product at considerable savings. Once they purchased and paid, he left them hanging. He took the money and ran.

If you own a business, run a business or work for a business that cheats, robs, steals, takes, beats, drains, depletes, harms, etc., in any way, it is wise for you to get out of that business.

The financial "success" of competitive profits is short-lived and/or erased by spiritual, mental, emotional relationships and physical disasters. The owner of the private phone company was out-of-business within two years. Many dissatisfied customers sued. The owner's attorney fees ate up all his profits.

"When you rise from the competitive to the creative plane, you can scan your business transactions very strictly, and if you are selling anyone anything which does not add more to their life than the thing they give you in exchange, you can afford to stop it. You do not have to beat anybody in business. And if you are in a business which does beat people, get out of it at once.

Give everyone more in use value than you take from them in cash value; then you are adding to the life of the world by every business transaction."

Wallace Wattles

Here's a practice that will assist you in continually aligning yourself with the creative forces. **Once you have counted what you have taken in, be sure to balance by reviewing what you have given out.**

Competition's Slaves, Creation's Masters.

Have you ever worked for a business where the atmosphere was filled with fear? Did you feel overly restricted, confined and limited? Did you feel like a slave?

A competitive business with its dualistic mentality (win/lose, success/failure, profit/loss, asset/liability, etc.,) automatically structures itself to make its employees into slaves.

Slaves have to be watched by slave drivers (competitive bosses, managers and executives) every minute of the work day to make sure they are doing what they're paid to do. Slaves require an inordinate number of rules to make sure they are productive workers. Slaves cannot think for themselves so slave drivers have to tell slaves what to do to make sure they always do things the "right" way.

Obviously for a business to make a profit the workers must produce more in cash value than you pay them in wages. That's where a competitive business and a MetaBusiness are similar.

They are different in that a competitive business is structured to keep a worker a slave and a MetaBusiness is structured to provide workers with opportunities for advancement. A competitive business uses fear to keep its workers on a competitive level. A MetaBusiness provides its workers with every opportunity to rise to the creative level and experience the freedom inherent in purpose.

In a competitive business, both the employer and employees have a slave mentality. In a MetaBusiness, the employer/employee co-creators have a "master" mentality. Here the word "master" is definitely not used in the "slave/master" context. Rather, it is used in the sense of a person being highly creative.

In a MetaBusiness, belief and mastery of the following is a priority. *"A Master can visualize persons, places, things and processes and then by impressing their thought/images upon formless substance can cause the persons, places, things and processes thought about to be created."* Wallace Wattles

Competition Excludes, Creation Includes

Visualize the following scenario. Mama's Restaurant has been doing a booming business for ten years. The owner, Betty Johnson, opened Mama's on a shoestring budget. She used her mother's recipes on the menu. Mama's swiftly became known for the best home cooking in town.

Then one day, Mother's, a national restaurant chain, bought land across the street and opened within three months. At this point let's watch Betty take two different paths.

Path 1

Betty is angry, fearful and depressed all at once on Mother's grand opening day. They spent thousands on television, radio and print advertising. A large grand opening sign covered half the building.

Mother's was packed. The large blacktop parking lot was nearly full. Mama's parking lot was only half as big. Some of their customers were parking in her lot and walking over to Mother's.

Betty flashed images of herself going out-of-business. She felt her loyal customers would go for the lower prices and faster service. She felt hopeless with the thought of competing with Mother's.

Path 2

Betty feels angry, fearful and slightly depressed all at once on Mother's grand opening. She decides not to dwell on the negative. Instead, she tells herself there's plenty of business for everyone. Besides, Mother's appeals to a different customer than Mama's.

At first Betty felt threatened by the media blitz but quickly realized without spending a penny that thousands of potential new customers would see Mama's across the street.

When Betty saw Mother's parking lot nearly full, she went over and introduced herself to the manager and offered to let Mother's use Mama's parking during the grand opening. The manager was so grateful, he offered to tell Betty about some food distributors which could save her an extra 10-15%.

Competition excludes, creation includes. A MetaBusiness transforms what appears to be a competitive conflict into creative cooperation.

The Mother's manager could have turned down Betty's help. The point is by including Mother's, she allowed the limitless energy to flow. By excluding Mother's, Betty cut off the flow from the limitless presence and fell to the fearful competitive level.

Competition Stagnates, Creation Innovates

A MetaBusiness is essentially "inner-oriented". Its primary focus is on "purpose". By purpose I mean there is a continuous focusing and refocusing on creating a product/service which enriches, benefits and improves the lives of everyone who purchases the product/service.

Since a competitive business operates from a warped fight-or-flight instinct, eventually the flight/fear phase of the cycle will attract stagnating energies. Often products/services will not be up-to-date. What has been successful in the past will be duplicated in the future. As a result, the products/services do not meet the present needs of customers/clients.

Flight/fear energies are attracted into the competitive businesses' environment. The owners, officers and employees begin to identify more and more intensely with emotions like panic, fear, escape, anger, depression, despair, and desperation.

No doubt about it, when a competitive business is in the fight phase it gives the appearance of growth, innovation and creation. The outer-oriented fight belief system leads inevitably to a stagnation cycle, flight and fear.

A MetaBusiness, on the other hand, operates from a creative purpose, inner-orientation. The fight (future) - flight (past) belief system is replaced by *awareness of the continuous changes in the present*.

Naturally a MetaBusiness is subject to alternating cycles of more and less. The difference is a MetaBusiness will usually not go through extreme ups and downs. In the "less", "down" cycle MetaBusiness owners, officers and employees (co-creators) will let go flight/fear feelings by refocusing on purpose.

Renewing purpose releases creative energies which produces innovative ideas, plans, processes and activities.

Summary of Chapter 3

1. The competitive life brings out conflicts, the "best" in one area, the "worst" in another. It brings imbalance, disharmony, one-sidedness and addictive behavior.

2. A MetaBusiness rejects competitive conflict in favor of cooperative creativity.

3. A MetaBusiness originates, creates a service and/or product which takes nothing away from anyone and takes advantage of no one.

4. Remember, just because you believe something does not mean you practice it consistently.

5. Focusing and identifying with a limited supply tunes you into feelings of lack, fear and eventually panic.

6. If you can communicate your thoughts to formless substance, you can cause the creation of "things" (events / services / processes / products) thought about.

7. Competition is fearful; creation is faithful. A MetaBusiness has faith in the creative process and knows how to put it into action.

8. As a MetaBusiness leader, you may from time to time become temporarily identified with lack; your fears may, for a time, blind you to the limitless supply making you focus on the apparent limited supply.

9. When that happens, stop focusing on the visible supply. Change the focus of your attention placing it in knowing faith on the limitless supply in formless substance.

10. A business that restricts, drains, frightens, punishes and generally leaves the customer/client with less life, health, happiness and love is on the competitive level.

11. A business that releases, energizes, enlightens, frees, and generally leaves the customer/client with more life, health, happiness and love is on the creative level. In short, competition takes and creation gives.

12. Once you have counted what you have received, be sure to balance by reviewing what you have given out.

13. A competitive business with its dualistic mentality (win/lose, success/failure, profit/loss, asset/liability, etc.) automatically structures itself to make its employees into slaves.

14. Obviously for a business to make a profit, the workers must produce more in cash value than you pay them in wages. That's where a competitive business and a MetaBusiness are similar.

15. A competitive business is structured to keep a worker a slave, and a MetaBusiness is structured to provide workers with opportunities for advancement. That's how they are different.

16. In a competitive business, both the employers and employees have a slave mentality. In a MetaBusiness, the employers/employees (co-creators) have a master mentality.

17. Competition excludes, creation includes. A MetaBusiness transforms what appears to be a competitive conflict into creative cooperation.

18. Inclusion allows the limitless energy to flow. Exclusion cuts off the flow from the limitless supply.

19. Since a competitive business operates from a fight-or-flight premise, eventually the flight/fear phase of the cycle will attract stagnant energies.

20. A MetaBusiness operates from a creative purpose. The fight (future), flight (past) belief system is replaced by awareness of continuous changes in the present.

21. In a "down" cycle a MetaBusiness' owners, officers and employees (co-creators), will let go of flight/fear feelings by refocusing on purpose.

22. Renewing purpose releases creative energies which produce innovative ideas, plans, processes and activities.

Chapter 4: Gratitude Replaces Greed

Feast, Famine and Greed

Being in business many years, I have heard myself say "It's either feast-or-famine." And I've heard many other business people say the same, " It's either feast-or-famine."

If your business has extreme cycles of either "feast" or "famine", it is likely you are subconsciously identified with the competitive levels. The "feast-or-famine" syndrome relates precisely with the "fight-or-flight" instinctive identification.

When a competitive business is in the famine cycle, the desire for the feast cycle becomes so intense that unbalanced behaviors tend to increase. Valuable business assets, for example, may be sold at a reduced price to raise money fast. If fear is the motivation, then chances are the panic sale will bring short-term benefits but long-term regrets.

Now, when a competitive business is in the feast cycle, greed begins to activate more intensely. Greed is the unbalanced urge for more, and then a clinging to more when it comes. This is when a competitive business is likely to over expand its operations in an attempt to avoid (fear) the next famine cycle.

Greed focuses obsessively on the limited supply. A competitive business likes to count what it has earned over and over again. It likes to broadcast its increased profits (feast cycle) repeatedly to impress others with its stockpile of resources.

One of the greatest difficulties with greed is that it blinds owners, business leaders, executives, and officers to need. They are so busy celebrating their success they do not see the new needs continuously arising in the present.

Of course, in the "famine/failure" cycle, competitive business leaders are obsessed on need. There's not enough capital, cash flow, help, time, space, and/or energy.

Have you ever been around a needy person? Yes! Then you know what a drain it is to be around them. You naturally feel it is wise to stay away.

A competitive (needy) business drains its employees, customers, suppliers, managers and owners. A starvation vortex pulls with such a compulsive force that those caught in its spin are obsessed with fear, lack, despair, craving, desire, and/or escape.

Institutional Greed

We have allowed something unfortunate to occur in our culture: "Institutional Greed". Our business, banking, political systems, etc., actually push and promote greed as a way of life. These institutions pride themselves on the intensity of their greed.

Greed is portrayed as an acceptable, even a superior way of life. To beat out the competitor, to take their market share, to buy them out covertly, are considered acceptable business practices.

Often, competitive business leaders, magazines, newspapers, television stations like to use competitive sports analogies: "The winning team; we scored a touch down; we out scored them; we hit a home run; they struckout". It's no accident that some of the greediest competitive business people are sports fanatics. It is no accident that professional sports is one of the greediest competitive business arenas.

Institutional greedy sports organizations begin early on. By 5, 6, and 7 years old, our children are indoctrinated with the "competitive spirit". Baseball, football, basketball, etc., leagues stress winning at all cost (notice the word "cost").

Greed is the unbalanced urge for more, and then a clinging to more when it comes. Many corporations, businesses, banking systems and national governments are "greed machines". They are like giant astral vacuums sucking up every dime they can get.

If you ever have the opportunity, visit the stock exchange. Notice your energies/feelings. The greed machine is plugged in, turned on and sucking for dear life.

As individuals, we must not gloss over, cover up or deny the institutional greed that pervades and permeates our societies. The greedier we become, the less grateful we are. The less grateful we are for the opportunities, experiences and rewards that have come into our lives the less creative we are as a civilization.

As a result, destructive forces are unleashed which increase the rate of decay, deterioration, and death of a civilization.

Stop giving institutional greed your acceptance and blessing. Give it no value. Begin focusing more and more on gratitude. Count your blessings. Align yourself with the creative source and the limitless supply in formless substance.

Greed Clings/Gratitude Gives

Programmed to get what we want through obsessive thought and desire, we cling internally to the image and hold on for dear life. When our greedy desire is fulfilled, we are successful and feel elated. When we do not get our desire, we are a failure and depressed.

Watch a young child in a toy store. Their desires are totally gripping. They have to have. When they do not get what they want, they often cry, scream, throw themselves on the floor, have a temper tantrum.

What do competitive individuals, competitive businesses do when they are not "successful", when they do not get the clinging (greedy) image/desires? Denial, blame, finger pointing, firing, cheating, stealing, escapism, etc. Destructive energies explode; what a temper tantrum!

MetaBusiness leaders focus more on gratitude and less on greed. Focusing on gratitude raises the vibration, lifting an individual out of the competitive frequencies and tuning them into the creative frequencies.

In a MetaBusiness there's a rhythmic renewal in thankfulness for the opportunity to create a service/product which not only gives others a genuine benefit but also generates financial rewards. Being grateful acknowledges the sources of opportunities, benefits and rewards.

Focusing on gratitude releases any attachments to "success" or "failure". As a result, a giving energy is released. A MetaBusiness is characterized by gratitude and giving. It asks the question, "What can we genuinely give our customers/clients out of gratitude for their purchases?"

Gratitude transforms greed into giving. Try it. Do it right now. You are grateful for.........? Feel it. Just thinking isn't going to do it. Feel it deeply.

Gratitude Affirms Abundance

If you're a MetaBusiness owner, how do you transmute the "lack frequency"? The "lack frequency" is the feeling you feel in the gut when you focus on the limited supply. There's not enough to pay the bills; there's not enough cash flow.

When you are intensely identified with lack, with the appearance of a limited supply, you plunge into the competitive level. Greed/need, feast/famine, fight/flight, are activated. The question then is: How do you detach and detune from the lack frequencies?

Step 1 Become acutely aware of the "lack frequency" the instant you feel it. Notice precisely where you feel it in and through your body. Notice the thoughts and images that accompany the "lack frequency".

Step 2 Stop feeding the "lack frequency" your energy. The more intensely you focus and feel the lack the more you feed it. Energy follows attention.

Step 3 Turn the focus of your attention to gratitude.

Focus on gratitude continuously. Be grateful for the little things, the big things, the successes and even the failures. Whatever you see, whatever you touch, whomever you are with be grateful. Be grateful for this and the words you are reading right now.

Step 4 Now that you have changed channels from the "lack frequency" to the "gratitude frequency", change channels again. Focus on the limitless supply in formless substance.

Gratitude leads to feelings of abundance. Gratitude affirms abundance.

Focus on the stars in the universe. Focus on the grains of sand on earth's beaches. Focus on the drops of water that fill the oceans. There is a limitless supply in formless substance.

Step 5 Pay attention to the creative thoughts, ideas, images, plans, and processes that arise spontaneously in your mind while focusing on abundance. They often give you the direction you need to take on a practical, day-to-day level to overcome/release the apparent lack predicament.

Step 6 Act on the creative plan. Often a new idea or process will trigger some apprehension. Go forward with awareness. Be willing to be uncomfortable. Persist in the creative process.

Step 7 Be grateful for the creative plan, for the privilege of putting it into action and the abundance that manifests. See/feel it already accomplished.

The Gratitude Break

As a MetaBusiness person, you must bring into your everyday consciousness deep and profound feelings of gratitude. Perhaps one way to remind yourself to give thanks is to set up "Gratitude Breaks".

A Gratitude Break is a specific time of day (or preferably several times a day) set aside to enjoy your connection to the limitless supply through the practice of gratitude.

Let's go through a gratitude break scenario to see how it might go.

Barbara owns and operates a sportswear manufacturing company. She goes into her office at 10:15 in the morning. The door is closed. Barbara has clearly requested her secretary to hold all calls for the next 15 minutes.

Barbara sits comfortably at her desk and takes a deep breath. She looks around her office. In her thoughts and feelings she acknowledges the limitless supply in heartfelt gratitude for the wonderful office space she has to work in.

She glances out the window and is grateful for the spectacular view of the soaring snowcapped Rocky Mountains. She is grateful for the substantial income her business provides. She is grateful for the many ski weekends she can easily afford.

Barbara's focus returns to the office. She is thankful for all her wonderful employees, for their expertise and commitment. She is thankful for the fabric suppliers who, for the most part, deliver the goods on time. She is thankful for all the wholesalers and retailers who recognize and appreciate the quality of her sportswear line.

Next, Barbara thinks of her family. She acknowledges her mother's designing and sewing skills and how they influenced her in childhood. Her husband is also a major source of support. She makes a point of thanking him daily for his suggestions, understanding and patience.

As Barbara's gratitude break winds down, she feels in harmony with the limitless supply. She expects, feels and visualizes more good things to happen. Barbara's faith in the power and creative process is renewed.

Gratitude Replaces Greed

As long as competitive leaders in all sectors of our "civilization" manipulate the supply and demand of goods and services in order to satisfy their greed, gratitude will not be culturally powerful. MetaBusiness leaders can and must take the initiative by introducing gratitude into their lives and businesses. Gradually, as more and more individuals experience the inner harmony of gratitude, gratitude will replace greed in the marketplace and eventually in other cultural systems.

Alfred Korzybski in 1933 clearly pointed out the fundamental differences between animal behavior and human behavior. Animals do not create more food, new inventions and greater knowledge.

In the animal world, the supply is limited. If there's not enough to go around, some do not survive. If there's not enough food, animals must fight/struggle to survive., The survival of the fittest instinct is structurally and functionally appropriate.

Humans, on the other hand, can create a limitless supply in formless substance. For example, 3% of the United States population feeds the other 97%. You will never see 3% of the animal kingdom feed the other 97%.

It is my contention that if enough of us begin to accept our structure and function as humans to consciously create rather than unconsciously imitate animals, we would detach ourselves from the survival of the fittest mentality. We would go beyond the two-valued, caught in the opposites, conflict which violates our human structure. Greed/need, supply/demand, fight/flight, feast/famine, etc., (all useful animal responses) will be replaced with creation, cooperation, purpose, gratitude and full recognition of the limitless supply in formless substance.

In a global culture motivated from gratitude rather than greed less than 1% of the population could produce more than enough food for the other 99%. This possibility does not appear to be in the near future. Greedy competitive leaders have their hands on the supply and demand spigots. Farmers, for example, are paid by competitive leaders not to grow crops, artificially manipulating supply and demand. The greedy are assured their profits.

As a MetaBusiness leader, practicing regular gratitude breaks, there's no need to over-analyze or obsess on the present problem; rather, he or she recognizes what's happening and then chooses to focus on gratitude and the limitless supply in formless substance. The competitive consciousness is replaced by the creative consciousness. Gratitude replaces greed.

Summary of Chapter 4

1. If your business has extremes cycles of either "feast-or-famine", it is likely you are subconsciously identifying with the competitive level.

2. When a competitive business is in the famine cycle, the desire for the feast cycle becomes so intense that unbalanced behaviors tend to increase.

3. When a competitive business is in the feast cycle, greed begins to activate more intensely. Greed is the unbalanced urge for more, and then a clinging to more when it comes.

4. A competitive (needy) business drains its employees, customers, suppliers, managers and owners. A starvation vortex pulls with such a compulsive force that those caught in its spin are obsessed with fear, lack, despair, craving, desire, and/or escape.

5. We have allowed something unfortunate to occur in our culture: "Institutional Greed". Our business, banking, political systems, etc., actually push and promote greed.

6. Many corporations, businesses, banking systems and national governments are "greed machines". They are like giant astral vacuums sucking up every dime they can get.

7. Stop giving institutional greed your acceptance and blessing. Give it no value. Begin focusing more and more on gratitude. Count your blessings. Align yourself with the creative frequencies.

8. Since we are immersed in a competitive society, we have been programmed to get what we want through obsessive thought and desire. We cling internally to the image/desire and hold on for dear life.

9. When our greedy desire is fulfilled, we are successful and elated. When we do not get our desire, we are a failure and depressed.

10. MetaBusiness leaders focus on gratitude. Focusing on gratitude raises the vibration, lifting an individual out of the competitive frequencies and tuning them into the creative frequencies.

11. Focusing on gratitude releases any attachments to "success" or "failure". As a result, a giving energy is released. A MetaBusiness is characterized by gratitude and giving.

12. When you are intensely identified with lack, with the appearance of a limited supply, you plunge into the competitive level. Greed/need, feast/famine, fight/flight, are activated.

13. How do you detach and detune from the lack frequencies?

Step 1 Become acutely aware.

Step 2 Stop focusing on lack.

Step 3 Focus your attention on gratitude.

Step 4 Focus on the limitless supply.

Step 5 Pay attention to creative thoughts.

Step 6 Act on the creative plan.

Step 7 Be grateful for the creative process and see/feel it already accomplished.

14. A Gratitude Break is a specific time of day (or preferably several times a day) set aside to enjoy your connection to the limitless supply in formless substance through the practice of gratitude.

15. Gradually, as more and more individuals experience the inner harmony of gratitude, gratitude will replace greed in the marketplace and eventually in other cultural systems.

16. In the animal world, the supply is limited. If there's not enough to go around, some do not survive. The survival of the fittest instinct is structurally and functionally appropriate.

17. Humans, on the other hand, can create a limitless supply out of formless substance. For example, 3% of the United States population feeds the other 97%. You will never see 3% of the animal kingdom feed the other 97%.

18. A MetaBusiness leader recognizes the competitive conflicts and then chooses to focus on gratitude and the limitless supply in formless substance.

19. Competitive greed is replaced by creative gratitude. Gratitude replaces greed.

Chapter 5: *Whole Living Replaces the Work Ethic*

The Work Ethic Competes

One of the primary reasons the competitively wealthy have amassed fortunes is the belief in the "work ethic". The work ethic is the belief that hard work, long hours and employer loyalty will be recognized and rewarded. The work ethic mind-set places the focus of waking life on work, hard work.

Taking pride in long, hard work (The Work Ethic) keeps a person on the competitive levels. Time and energy for play, creativity and spirituality seems to evaporate. One-sided, unbalanced living becomes a virtue.

I recently heard on the radio that Japan has surpassed the United States in total net worth, in the trillions of dollars. Is that bad news for the U.S.? From the competitive level the answer is yes. From the creative level the answer is no. To me it is good news. Being Number One is a work ethic, competitive level obsession which leads to unbalanced behaviors physically, emotionally, and mentally.

According to a Japanese friend, the Japanese are working longer and harder. They are producing more, saving more and investing more. On the other hand, he pointed out, the spiritual and creative traditions have disintegrated.

In recent years, work ethic believers in the United States have found out the sad truth. Competitive leaders are more interested in profits than in people. Steel workers, airline workers, electronic workers, clothing workers . . . by the millions, hard working people with 10, 20, 30 or more years with a company are without a paycheck.

An increase in divorce, crime, addictions, suicides, depression, etc., followed. The work ethic belief system is too rigid and unbalanced. Since so much of the life emphasis is on work, when unexpected difficult circumstances arise, creative and spiritual qualities are not developed enough to handle the adversities.

The standard of living has risen to the point that it takes two incomes (two hard workers) to support house, car, insurance, food, clothing, etc. If the greedy competitive leaders had their way, it would take three, four and five hard working people to buy a house, a car, and health insurance.

Fortunately, work ethic believers by the millions are wising up. A well-rounded lifestyle that includes creativity and spirituality, Whole Living, is fast replacing the competitive work ethic.

Whole Living Creates.

Look at the Wheel of Whole Living, figure 3 below.

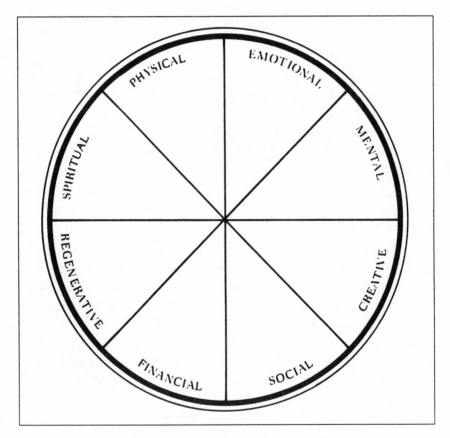

Figure 3: Wheel of Whole Living

Here a person's life energies are divided into eight different areas. Naturally, in daily life all areas are intimately and dynamically interconnected and interactive. Let me give a short description of each life energy.

PHYSICAL — Exercise, nutrition, fresh air, hygiene, restful sleep, relaxation, recreation, health maintenance, sex, etc.

EMOTIONAL — Likes, dislikes, fears, anger, desires, subconscious blocks, pressure points, semantic reactions, identifications, attachments, possessiveness, etc.

MENTAL — Words, images, thoughts, concepts, speech, communication, ideas, thinking, reading, learning, concentration, focus, etc.

CREATIVE — Art, music, dance, color, light, form, beauty, drama, crafts, play, painting, drawing, sculpting, design, etc.

SOCIAL — Relationships, love, networking, communication, cooperation, sharing, caring, etc.

FINANCIAL — Money, investment, banking, prosperity, wealth, income, saving, spending, buying, paying, earning, etc.

REGENERATIVE — Relaxation, meditation, massage, releasing, transmuting, resting, taking breaks, rhythmic breathing, recharging, etc.

SPIRITUAL — Tuning to the source, experiencing the divine presence, feeling peace in the chaos, silence on the non-verbal level, light, love, humor, joy, understanding, wisdom, etc.

Entire chapters could be devoted to each life energy. Here, I want you to get a "feel" for each. (See *Tuning to the Spiritual Frequencies* by Greg Nielsen).

As a MetaBusiness person, you place value on whole living. You live dynamically, giving your attention, time and energy to each life energy as you rhythmically sense its natural need and expression.

A wonderful and miraculous process unfolds. You experience whole living which stabilizes you on the creative level. Nothing casts you into the competitive energy levels faster than unwhole, unbalanced, one-sided, one-dimensional behaviors.

When a MetaBusiness person experiences difficulties, frustrations, blockages, or losses, he or she looks to the Wheel of Whole Living and recognizes where the imbalance lies. Next, he or she takes action to gain equilibrium. If in recent days and weeks, she or he has not taken enough time to rest, relax and regenerate, she or he has a massage, takes an extra day off or goes away for a relaxing weekend.

Becoming an Energy Being

We are going through an evolutionary shift in consciousness on our planet. This evolutionary shift is one hundredfold greater than the consciousness change after the discovery of fire.

For untold thousands of years the vast majority of people alive on this planet at any given time were, for the most part, identified with rigid mind-sets, belief systems, dogmas, philosophies, ideologies, creeds, codes, rules, laws, religions, etc. To some degree each of these fixed mind-maps worked. They guided, to some extent, the lives of the individuals who valued them, identified with them and believed them.

Where are all the societies, cultures and civilizations today which believed these various mind-maps? They disintegrated. Only remnants remain. They were doomed to destruction because the map is never the territory. To identify the map with the territory guarantees eventual non-survival.

Right now, and into the 21st Century, we are in the midst of an evolutionary shift in consciousness away from fixed mind-maps to becoming conscious of energy. We are becoming Energy Beings sensitive and aware of super-subtle, subtle and not-so-subtle changes in the rates of vibration of people, places and things in the outer space-time-energy-matter environment and inner thought-feeling-emotion-sensation environment.

MetaBusiness leaders are becoming Energy Beings. To be a MetaBusiness leader, by definition, you must be an Energy Being. The way I see it now, in most cases, **it is a 3 to 7 year persistent commitment to make the evolutionary shift in daily practice from non-survival fixed mind-maps to survival Energy Being consciousness.**

MetaBusiness leaders live and breathe as Energy Beings, maintaining the creative levels. Their identification and belief in the fixed mind-map, survival of the fittest, fight/flight, need/greed, supply/demand, feast/famine etc., is progressively and geometrically given less and less value. They value most the awareness of the energy dynamics in the present of every process, place, person, product, and service.

With present energy awareness, possibilities and choices are broadened. Flexibility and adaptability are natural behaviors of a functioning Energy Being. An Energy Being knows from experience that energy follows attention. **Therefore, they pay attention to their attention.**

Efficient Action

If you are interested in living a balanced, whole life, you will not have the time or energy to "work hard", to overwork. Whole living requires efficient action, not "hard work". As a MetaBusiness person, emphasize efficient action, not long hours.

Efficient action demands awareness. When you do too many things in too short a time, two behaviors inevitably occur: (1) your awareness level drops into unconsciousness, (2) your actions are inefficient. Unconscious, inefficient activities lead automatically into the competitive levels. Inefficient activity breeds conflict, struggle, panic, fear, greed, need and failure.

The MetaBusiness person who is living from wholeness is living with awareness. Her or his actions must, as a result, be efficient. In a MetaBusiness, a minimum of activity generates maximum financial returns.

I can give you an example from my own business experience of how an efficient activity generated a substantial financial return.

One day I felt intuitively (awareness) that it would be wise to send a copy of one of my books to a foreign publisher. I followed through on that awareness by writing a letter and mailing a book that day. It took about one-half hour, efficient action.

Within three weeks my foreign publishing representative received a letter from the same publisher offering a $1,500 advance. In another week I had a contract on my desk which I reviewed and signed within another half hour. One hour has generated $1,500.00 so far. Once the book is published, sales may generate several more thousands of dollars for that one hour of efficient action.

As Wattles writes, *"It is really not the number of things you do, but the efficiency of each separate action that counts."*

If you're working too hard and/or rushing too much, more than likely you are operating your business on a competitive level. Please do not misunderstand me. I am not saying you should never put in long hours or rush. Naturally there may be times when it is required. What I am saying is long hours and rushing are an inefficient way to run a business.

Reexamine your business on a regular basis looking for ways to operate it more efficiently. Look for minimum effort creating maximum financial returns.

Efficient action in your MetaBusiness creates free time to read, travel, play, relax and tune into the limitless supply. Whole living replaces the work ethic.

Doing Nothing.

For most, the work ethic is so deeply ingrained in the mind-body that slowing down, taking time off, calling-in sick or just "doing nothing" is out of the question. Many feel guilty if they are not doing or accomplishing something. I call this dis-ease Americanitis.

Whole living requires time for regeneration, relaxation, rest, recreation, rejuvenation and just "doing nothing". The Chinese Taoist philosophers have a term for "doing nothing", wu-wei (woo-way). Literally, the translation means "non-action".

Chuang-Tzu writes, "*Non-action does not mean doing nothing and keeping silent. Let everything be allowed to do what it naturally does, so that its nature will be satisfied.*" Lao Tzu said it this way, "*By nonaction everything can be done.*"

Work ethic, competitive level owners, leaders and workers cannot comprehend non-action, wu-wei, just plain "doing nothing...". It feels uncomfortable, impossible, ridiculous, and absurd. When I suggest "doing nothing" to those who are smitten with Americanitis, they look aghast, horrified, uptight, and/or hostile.

The work ethic mind-set does not include "doing nothing" to accomplish something. The work ethic mind-set believes you must always be doing something in order to accomplish something.

A budding MetaBusiness person called me in a frenzy. She was in conflict over what she was going to do on her one week vacation (her potential wu-wei time). I asked if she had to make a decision in the next 48 hours. She said no. I suggested she do nothing, think nothing, and say nothing regarding her vacation decision for the next 48 hours.

I could tell this idea of doing nothing seemed out of the question at first. Mentally-emotionally-physically, she was so identified with the urgency of making an immediate decision that it felt almost impossible to believe doing nothing could lead to an answer without all the struggle.

She did do her best to drop her anxiety about her vacation time. The decision fell more or less into place without a lot of anguish, obsessive thinking and compulsive doing (competitive level activities).

A MetaBusiness appreciates and practices "doing nothing" as long as it comes from whole living, not irresponsibility and laziness. Those times of restful inactivity become the source of spontaneous creative thought which often are the impetus for more efficient activities.

Making Time

Many on the competitive levels (mostly unconsciously and automatically) divide their time into two segments: (1) work and (2) sleep. Eventually, as competition leads into the fight/success cycle with more money to spend, a third time segment arises which might be called "competitive play".

The workaholic is an obvious example of a dualistic work/sleep competitive type. In fact, in extreme workaholism (work ethic insanity) there is a feeling that there is no time for rest, relaxation and sleep. Often these insane workaholics will take stimulants to prevent rest, relaxation and sleep.

There are millions upon millions of threefold work/sleep/play competitive types. Their play time is not on the creative level. It is competitive play. Baseball, football, hockey, tennis, golf, basketball, boxing, soccer.... The list goes on and on. Conflict, tension and struggle - the competitive dualistic mentality continues into playtime.

Whole living is multi-dimensional. A MetaBusiness person makes time for whatever activities are necessary for balance. Whole living is on a creative level.

Creative play replaces competitive play. Creative playtime is characterized by enjoyment, cooperation, spontaneity, increased energy, lack of criticism, greater awareness and feelings of wholeness.

Often the work ethic types will say, "I don't have time to relax", "I don't have time to read", "I don't have time to solve my personal problems", "I don't have time for creative hobbies", "I don't have time to meditate".

Of course the work ethic type never has enough time. Whole, balanced living is not acceptable based on their dualistic belief system: work/sleep, fight/flight, feast/famine.

A MetaBusiness encourages the creative individual's participation in the continuous creation of the business, making time for relaxation, reading, self-development, creativity, and meditation. In fact, a MetaBusiness would be well advised to inform its creators of whole living events, programs and activities on local, regional, national and international levels.

It would be wise for a MetaBusiness to provide space and make time for relaxation, meditation, reading, creative play, etc. MetaBusinesses are now creating Energy Rooms for rejuvenation through alpha wave music, color therapy, brain wave machines, relaxation biocircuits, aromatherapy, art therapy, massage therapy, and health maintenance.

Summary of Chapter 5

1. Taking pride in long, hard work (the work ethic) keeps a person on the competitive levels.

2. The work ethic belief system is too rigid and unbalanced. Since so much of the life emphasis is on work, when unexpected difficult circumstances arise, creative and spiritual qualities are not developed enough to handle the adversities.

3. Fortunately, work ethic believers by the millions are wising up. A well-rounded lifestyle that includes creativity and spirituality, Whole Living, is fast replacing the competitive work ethic.

4. A person's life energies can be divided into eight different areas: Physical, emotional, mental, creative, social, financial, regenerative, and spiritual. Naturally, in daily life all areas are interconnected and interactive.

5. As a MetaBusiness person you place value on Whole Living. You live dynamically, giving your attention, time and energy to each life energy as you rhythmically sense its natural need.

6. Right now we are in the midst of an evolutionary shift in consciousness away from fixed mind-maps to becoming conscious of energy.

7. We are becoming Energy Beings, sensitive and aware of super-subtle, subtle and not-so-subtle changes in the rates of vibration of people, places and things in the outer space-time-energy-matter environment and inner thought-feeling-emotion-sensation environment.

8. An Energy Being knows from experience that Energy Follows Attention. *Therefore, they pay attention to their attention.*

9. If you are interested in living a balanced, whole life you will not have the time or energy to "work hard" to overwork! Whole Living requires efficient action not "hard work". As a MetaBusiness person, emphasize efficient action, not long hours.

10. Efficient action demands awareness. When you do too many things in too short a time, two behaviors inevitably occur: (1) your awareness level drops into unconsciousness (2) your actions are inefficient.

11. Unconscious, inefficient actions lead automatically into the competitive levels. Inefficient activity breeds, conflict, struggle, panic, fear, greed, need and failure.

12. The MetaBusiness person who is living from wholeness is living with awareness. Her or his actions must, as a result, be efficient. In a MetaBusiness, a minimum of activity generates maximum financial returns.

13. Efficient action in your MetaBusiness creates free time to read, travel, play, relax and tune into the limitless supply. Whole Living replaces the work ethic.

14. For most, the work ethic is so deeply ingrained in the mind-body that slowing down, taking time off calling-in sick or just "doing nothing" is out of the question.

15. Many feel guilty if they are not doing or accomplishing something. I call this dis-ease Americanitis.

16. The Chinese Taoist philosophers have a term for "doing nothing", wu-wei (woo-way). Literally, the translation means "non-action". Lao Tzu said it this way, *"By non-action everything can be done."*

17. A MetaBusiness person appreciates and practices "doing nothing" as long as it comes from Whole Living, not irresponsibility and laziness. Those times of restful inactivity become the source of spontaneous creative thought which often are the impetus for more efficient activities.

18. The workaholic is an obvious example of a dualistic work/sleep competitive type. In fact, in extreme workaholism (work ethic insanity) there is a feeling that there is no time for rest, relaxation and sleep.

19. In Whole Living, creative play replaces competitive play. Creative playtime is characterized by enjoyment, cooperation, spontaneity, increased energy, lack of criticism, greater awareness and feelings of wholeness.

20. A MetaBusiness encourages the creative individual's participation in continuous creation of the business, making time for relaxation, reading, self-development, creativity, and meditation.

Chapter 6: Rhythm Replaces Rush

Competition Rushes

A business is on the competitive level if the employees are continuously rushing. There never seems to be enough time. Often the owners are trying to squeeze every drop of energy out of an employee for the time paid for.

What happens when you do too many things in too short a time by rushing?

- Quality diminishes.
- Actions are inefficient.
- Accidents increase.
- Emotional conflicts increase.
- Stress and tensions increase.
- Disease and sickness increases.
- Customer satisfaction decreases.
- Employee fears rise.
- Job satisfaction decreases.
- Quality employees leave.
- Present awareness diminishes.
- Customer loyalty wanes.
- Sales drop.
- Profits go down.
- Mistakes have to be corrected.
- Time is wasted
- Etc.

The competitive rush mentality is deeply ingrained. In fact, it appears to be "perfectly normal". Missed deadlines, last minute changes, forgotten details are common events in a competitive business addicted to the rush mentality.

The mass media is a whirlwind of rush. Visit your daily newspaper. There is rush in the air. Radio and television news comes in at such a fast rate that news writers, newscasters, and news producers rush madly trying to keep up.

Our political leaders, especially on the campaign trail, rush like mad bees from one rally to the next. It's perfectly acceptable behavior to rush like a maniac. Often voters give high marks to a candidate that can rush day in and day out without appearing tired. As long as we value rush, our leaders will be on the competitive level.

Our educational system has students dashing from one class to another. Learn more, memorize more, study more. An intellectual pride that values much learning in a short time, guarantees that our education will be competitive.

No wonder our businesses are obsessed with competitive rush. "Hurry up or someone else will beat you to it!" is the watch phrase of many competitive business leaders. Be one step ahead of the competition. You must have the competitive edge. The fear that the competition will do it before you do pushes the rush button.

As individuals, one by one, begin to devalue rush and value rhythm, our cultural addiction to competitive rush will be replaced by creative rhythms. A MetaBusiness encourages creative rhythms.

Creative Rhythms

A MetaBusiness does not rush its employees. A MetaBusiness does not rush its service. A MetaBusiness does not rush the manufacturing process.

A MetaBusiness thrives in an environment which is sensitive and responsive to creative rhythms. Let's say, for example, an employee is tired or even drained. A MetaBusiness would allow the person to respond to the tiredness by resting. (A creative rhythm)

Perhaps a room is provided for relaxation, rest, rejuvenation and naps. A short nap of ten to thirty minutes will more than likely increase the quality of the employees' actions.

In fact, the word "employee" is not an accurate label for those participating in a MetaBusiness. The competitive/slave associations attached to the word "employee" run deep. In fact, the word employee has the word "ploy" within it indicating trickery. Co-Creator is functionally a more accurate description of MetaBusiness employees.

If a MetaBusiness "co-creator" has a particular set of tasks she or he is responsible for, she or he accepts the responsibility and does it. On the other hand, if a co-creator feels that she or he is getting into a rut, a MetaBusiness encourages, expects and accepts the co-creator focusing on other tasks.

Perhaps MetaBusinesses could establish exchange systems whereby co-creators could apply for task exchanges with other co-creators. The time factor could vary from a few minutes a day, to weeks, to a total job exchange. In this way a MetaBusiness responds to the natural creative rhythms of living, breathing co-creators.

A MetaBusiness is responsive to the changing energy rhythms. A co-creator may begin doing one set of tasks, but in time may end up doing an entirely different set through a natural process.

In a competitive business "employees" are viewed for the most part, as machines programmed with fixed job tasks to be repeated over and over. In a MetaBusiness "co-creators" are viewed as living energy beings uniquely experiencing events, and, therefore, responding differently to repeated tasks from one day to the next.

"Co-creators" may go about their appointed tasks, routinely achieving what is required to keep the MetaBusiness manifesting its purpose. Perhaps one day that "co-creator" is inspired by a creative plan which would improve a product or service. A MetaBusiness encourages this creative rhythm.

A MetaBusiness would expect the "co-creator" to take time at the earliest opportunity to write the plan down or record it on tape. Then, after putting it through a review process with other co-creators, the originator would be encouraged to evolve and implement the plan.

Rhythms

The Pattern of all Rhythms is illustrated by the solid line wave in figure 4 on page 6-4.

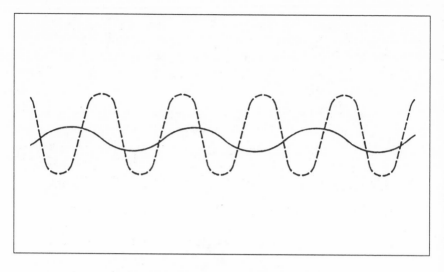

Figure 4: Pattern of All Rhythms

Try to find anything that does not exhibit rhythmic behavior. So far I have not found anything that does not have a rhythmic pattern.

You breathe in; you breathe out. The tide goes in; the tide goes out. The sun rises; the sun sets. The moon waxes; the moon wanes.

Rhythms abound in the business world as well. Sales increase; sales decrease. Cash flow goes up; cash flow goes down. Interest rates go up; interest rates go down. The Dow Jones average is up; the Dow Jones average is down.

A competitive business tends to be extreme in its rhythms illustrated by the dash wave above. In Chapter 4: "Gratitude Replaces Greed" the extreme swings between fight/flight and feast/famine were described.

A MetaBusiness, on the other hand, is illustrated by the solid wave. Those working in a MetaBusiness are encouraged to become sensitive and responsive to the natural energy rhythms in their daily activities. A MetaBusiness recognizes and acknowledges the rhythmic patterns in nature and the universe and strives to live in harmony with these natural rhythms.

Competitive businesses often unconsciously reject the fact that all life is rhythmic, and competitive businesses want only success, profits, and increased sales. They often deny the existence of the negative swing of the wave. As a result, they set themselves up for extreme failure, losses, and decreased sales.

It is important to see and understand that the "ups" are directly related to the "downs" just as mountains are connected to the valleys. A MetaBusiness owner understands the natural rhythmic relationship between the "ups" and "downs" and consciously chooses not to overly identify with either. Instead, she or he "goes with the flow".

Rhythmic Alternation

In order for a MetaBusiness to stabilize on the creative level and detune from the competitive frequencies, it must stop rushing. By practicing rhythmic alternation in all phases of the business the compulsive rush is eliminated.

Specifically, what is meant by rhythmic alternation? Rhythmic alternation requires awareness of energy cycles, sensitivity to energy cycle changes and wise responses to the changes in energy flow. So what happens on a day-to-day business level?

Employees, workers, MetaBusiness co-creators are first of all encouraged to be aware of their energy levels, whether energized, tired, depressed, drained, relaxed, mellow, or hyper. Those creating the MetaBusiness on a day-to-day basis must be conscious of their energy level from minute-to-minute, hour-to-hour, day-to-day, week-to-week.

This consciousness of energy cycles, flows and currents is critical because it creates an environment more attuned to the rhythmic cycles of body-mind-spirit.

The more individuals in a MetaBusiness practicing rhythmic alternation in their life, the more rhythmic the MetaBusiness. Rhythmic alternation is simple. When you're tired, you rest. When you're hungry, you eat. When you've been thinking too much, you stop thinking. When you're thirsty, you drink. When you've been working too much, you play.

Rhythmic alternation is as natural as breathing. In fact, a MetaBusiness encourages rhythmic breathing methods to enhance relaxation, awareness and productivity.

A MetaBusiness environment where rhythmic alternation is the natural way is highly charged with creative energy. The individuals within the MetaBusiness are actually energized by being around each other.

In a competitive business environment where rush is the norm, the energy goes through extreme ups and downs, hyper one minute, drained the next.

As much as possible a MetaBusiness creates a work schedule which is rhythmic. Time and energy are not separate. Time-energy are in reality inexplicably interactive.

In a competitive business, time is over-valued. The clock punching mentality is unrhythmic. Responsiveness to energy rhythms is hardly valued at all.

In a MetaBusiness, time-energy are valued together. Doing a particular task every day at the same time may not be possible in a MetaBusiness. Maybe the energy flows ahead of time or after the time. As a result, the task is completed with quality energy.

Mini-Rhythms

There are millions of people on the competitive level in their work life who are feeling the need to shift into a creative level but feel powerless to make that change. The demands on their time-energy in the competitive work environment leave little time-energy for creative level awareness and activities. At least, that's how they feel.

Not long ago I consulted with a high-powered competitive level business woman who was feeling that there had to be a better way. She is the mother of two children, divorced, commutes two hours a day and works a full eight hour day with little time for breaks or lunch.

When I brought up the possibility of rhythmic alternation as a practical way to transform her work consciousness from the competitive to the creative level, she responded as expected. "I don't have any time." Have you ever heard yourself say that? Yes? At that time you are burning-out on the rush frequencies. The competitive mind-set just doesn't work for you any more.

I asked the woman if it would be all right with her if we reviewed her day to see what time she might have for mini-rhythms. A mini-rhythm is a short cycle of rhythmic alternation. She agreed. She was willing to try anything. The stress and tension levels were wearing her out mentally, emotionally and physically.

I asked her what she did with the time driving to and from work (two hours). She said; "Think about what I'm going to do at work, think about problems with money, with children, with a new man friend".

I suggested she change the energy of that two hours by using her car cassette to listen to music and voice tapes. She responded immediately with, "Yes, that's a great idea".

She purchased numerous tapes which she felt were uplifting and inspirational and gave her a higher quality energy. Her drive time became a mini-rhythm of relaxation, rest, peace, calm and rejuvenation.

Next, I asked about her lunch time. She was supposed to take an hour each day. But she usually grabbed a sandwich and ate at her desk while taking calls. I suggested that she had that hour coming and she should take it no matter what.

She had the "work ethic" mentality. She was too responsible. I suggested she plan her lunch time for herself, going somewhere quiet like the nearby park where she could commune with nature. Also, if she brought her lunch, she would save the time of waiting for her lunch to be prepared.

These two mini-rhythmic alternation suggestions made a tremendous difference in this woman's energy. Before, she felt she had no time. Now she has three hours a day for herself. During that time she slows down, changes the focus of her attention and alternates from rush to rhythm.

Putting on the Brakes

"Do all that you can do in a perfect manner every day, but do it without haste, worry or fear. Go as fast as you can, but never hurry. Remember that in the moment you begin to hurry you cease to be a creator and become a competitor; you drop back upon the old plane again."

Wallace Wattles

When you start doing too many tasks in too short a time, you tune into the competitive frequencies. Never underestimate the power of the competitive frequencies. The mental-emotional energy levels are inundated by the endless onslaught of competitive messages.

Television, radio, newspapers, magazines, movies, and videos bombard the mental-emotional levels 24-hours a day, 365-days a year with the competitive message. The powers behind the competitive belief systems are unrelenting. They operate from fear. In their hearts, they are afraid they will lose their competitive edge. You must understand the power of the competitive frequencies have been built-up over hundreds if not thousands of years.

When you start to rush, you open yourself up to the competitive frequencies. Even if you have the best of intentions, rushing will sooner or later shift you into a competitive vortex of activity motivated by fear, worry, and doubt.

As a MetaBusiness person you have to know when to put on the brakes and slow down. You have to know when to put on the brakes and come to a complete stop.

As long as the competitive force has the upper hand, it is wise to practice vigilance. Learn and practice the art of self-observation. At least every 10-15 minutes throughout the day observe what is going on with yourself mentally, emotionally, and physically.

If you are fearful, anxious, nervous, hyper, and/or worried, you are emotionally in the competitive frequencies. Put on the emotional brakes, slow down, stop. Take a two hour lunch, go home early, take an extra day off. Take rhythmic action to let go of the competitive emotions.

If you observe your body and feel excess tensions, stiffness and rigidity, you have physically tuned into the competitive frequencies. You need to alternate into relaxation. Perhaps meditation, a massage, using the relaxation circuits (mentioned in chapter 10 in *Tuning to the Spiritual Frequencies* by Greg Nielsen) will release competitive tensions.

If you notice yourself thinking and speaking too fast, mentally obsessing on business "problems", thinking negatively, mentally you are on the competitive frequencies. Put on the mental brakes. Change the focus of your attention. Take a walk in the woods, by the beach...listen to the birds, the waves, the wind. Realign yourself with the creative power (the limitless supply in formless substance) by practicing gratitude, contemplating your vision, and acknowledging your purpose.

Summary of Chapter 6

1. As individuals begin to devalue rush and value rhythm, our cultural addiction to competitive rush will be replaced by creative rhythms.

2. A MetaBusiness thrives in an environment which is sensitive and responsive to creative rhythms.

3. In a competitive business "employees" are viewed for the most part as machines programmed with fixed job tasks to be repeated over and over. In a MetaBusiness "co-creators" are viewed as living energy beings uniquely experiencing events, and, therefore, responding differently to repeated tasks from one day to the next.

4. Perhaps a "co-creator" is inspired by a creative plan which would improve a product or service. A MetaBusiness encourages this creative rhythm.

5. A MetaBusiness recognizes and acknowledges the rhythmic patterns in nature and the universe and strives to live in harmony with these natural rhythms.

6. It is important to see and understand that the "ups" are directly related to the "downs" just as mountains are connected to the valleys.

7. A MetaBusiness leader understands the natural rhythmic relationship between the "ups" and "downs" and consciously chooses not to overly identify with either. Instead, she or he "goes with the flow."

8. In order for a MetaBusiness to stabilize on the creative level and detune from the competitive frequencies, it must stop rushing. By practicing rhythmic alternation in all phases of the business the compulsive rush is eliminated.

9. Rhythmic alternation requires awareness of energy cycle changes and wise responses to the changes in energy flow. This consciousness of energy cycles, flows and currents is critical because it creates an environment more attuned to the rhythmic cycles of body - mind - spirit.

10. A MetaBusiness environment where rhythmic alternation is the natural way is highly charged with creative energy. The individuals within the MetaBusiness are actually energized by being around each other.

11. In a competitive business environment where rush is the norm, the energy goes through extreme ups and downs, hyper one minute, drained the next.

12. When you start doing too many tasks in too short a time, you tune into the competitive frequencies. Never underestimate the power of the competitive frequencies. The mental-emotional levels are inundated by the endless onslaught of competitive messages.

13. When you start to rush, you open yourself up to the competitive frequencies. Even if you have the best of intentions, rushing will sooner or later sweep you into a competitive vortex of activity motivated by fear, worry, and doubt.

14. As a MetaBusiness person, you have to know when to put on the brakes and slow down. You have to know when to put on the brakes and come to a complete stop.

15. As long as the competitive forces have the upper hand it is wise to practice vigilance. Learn and practice the art of self-observation. At least every 10-15 minutes throughout the day observe what is going on with yourself mentally, emotionally and physically.

16. Take time to realign yourself with the creative power (the limitless supply in formless substance) by practicing gratitude, contemplating your vision and acknowledging your purpose.

Chapter 7: Intuition Complements Intellect

What Is Intellect?

The primary function of the intellect is to separate. In the business world the intellect is used to separate facts and figures. Without the analyzing capabilities of the intellect the business world as we know it would disappear. Without the developed intellect our economic system would return to hunting, fishing and trading. In fact, in many parts of the world where there is minimal intellectual development hunting, fishing and trading are the economic base.

Now this is in no way a judgment against non-intellect economic systems. I am not making the assumption here that our "modern" system is better or superior to their "primitive" system. Each system is appropriate to its time-place. Each has its positives and negatives as do most systems.

Our educational system focuses primarily on intellectual development. Those who can temporarily remember facts and figures at test time are usually rewarded with higher paying jobs. Our educational and economic systems emphasize intellectual development and generally de-emphasize other abilities like intuition, instinct, awareness, creativity, manual dexterity, sensitivity, spirituality, etc.

On the positive side, the intellect has led us into a technological age which reached its pinnacle with the computer. In many ways the computer is an electronic intellect. It separates facts and figures and remembers them better than us.

On the negative side the over-valuing of intellectual development has led to unbalanced behaviors on individual, community, national and international levels. A runaway intellect seems not to know when to stop separating. There's a strong tendency to lock into dualistic thinking. Success / failure, capitalism / socialism, democracy / communism, good / bad, right / wrong, win / lose ... the list continues ad infinitum.

When the "us versus them" mentality runs wild, we are left with the possibility of total self-destruction by splitting (separating) the atom. Our intellectual technology has brought us to the brink of annihilation. Faced with extinction, even the most prideful intellect begins to examine, think about other possibilities.

Learning to separate can be balanced with learning to bring together. Intellectual duality can be balanced with intuitive unity. The intellect has a wonderful, practical, life enriching capability when it is not over-developed.

A Competitive Business Over-Uses Intellect

As a business owner, leader or decision maker you have more than likely been up in the middle of the night thinking about what you should do. Your mind races with all kinds of possibilities, "what if's" and scenarios. Your thinking is usually connected with emotions like worry, fear, panic, apprehension, anger, and doubt.

In a competitive business which is based on fear... fight/flight, feast/famine, success/failure... the excessive thinking is often allied with negative emotions. Excessive negative thinking/emotion drains a lot of life energy.

Once you get into the habit of overusing the intellect... thinking obsessively about your work... you fall into the competitive level. At that point the stress and tension increase dramatically. In proportion, the quality of your business decisions decreases dramatically.

One of the things I've noticed in my business and, no doubt, you have noticed in your business, in recent years there has been a staggering increase in choices. Years ago most business practices were fairly standard. One step followed another as routinely as day follows night.

Today, with the information explosion, the intellect overloads, short-circuits with an endless current of words, images and concepts. As a result, simple and routine business practices have become outdated. New information means more possibilities, means more choices.

On the competitive level you try to "figure out" the best choice. You think about all the permutations and combinations. It takes a lot of time and energy. Often this "figuring out" decision-making process leads to confusion.

When the level of confusion becomes overwhelming, competitive leaders turn to so called experts and consultants. Sometimes the experts can narrow down the intelligent choices, but the final decisions still are the responsibility of the business leader.

In Chapter 5, I stated that we are in the midst of an evolutionary shift in consciousness away from fixed mind-maps (intellectual thinking) to becoming conscious of energy. Thinking requires energy. Excessive thinking uses up an unbalanced measure of energy.

From a Whole Living viewpoint, excessive thinking robs other life functions of their required energies. When you think too much, the body overloads with tension. This in turn drains physical vitality which lowers the immune system's power to resist dis-ease.

If you can identify with what has been said in this section, you may want to consider additional ways of decision making. Getting off the competitive levels and into the creative MetaBusiness levels can be assisted by using intuition in the decision-making process.

What is Intuition?

One Sunday morning I went out to buy the Sunday paper. It was a warm, lazy day. As I drove to the store I took my time. I noticed the rich green pine tree colors. I heard the morning songs of sparrows and whippoorwills.

Looking ahead I saw a stoplight turn green. The speed limit was 30 mph. Usually I would have accelerated through the light. Instead, I felt like taking my time. Actually, I slowed down slightly to look at the beauty of a riverside park.

Just before I got to the intersection, a car raced through a red light from my left at about 50 mph. Do you see what happened? If I had not intuitively felt like slowing down, there would have been a serious accident.

What is intuition? From one point of view, intuition is awareness of information not immediately available through seeing, hearing, touching, tasting and smelling.

As I mentioned in the first part of this chapter, the information explosion has drastically increased the possible choices. At some point the intellect overloads. It can handle only so many bits of data before it short-circuits. You feel overwhelmed and confused.

In a business environment, decisions must be made with clarity and wisdom. Often, decisions must be made immediately. Here's where the intuition comes in. Being sensitive to the feelings you're picking up on and then recognizing their validity is part of the intuitive process.

Consciously cultivating sensitivity to feelings, flash thoughts and hunches will give you a valuable tool for decision-making in your business or profession. Later in this chapter I will give you some specific ways to awaken, develop and enhance your intuitive awareness.

In recent years, intuitive decision-making has been more accepted. This became clear to me when I met the dean of a large university business college at a "Drawing of the Right Side of the Brain" class. The right brain functions are related to creativity, feeling, sensitivity, and intuition.

He told me, "*A business leader must use right brain intuitive skills along with left brain intellectual skills in order to be successful. Intellect alone will not get she or he very far. I strongly recommend to all my MBAs (Masters of Business Administration) that they take this course.*"

Balancing Intuition/Intellect

Let's make up a business called the Zeep Company. Mr. Zee feels (intuition) very strongly that his "zeep" will benefit people (purpose) both mentally and physically. The "zeep" is a small electronic device which prints out inspiring, motivating and encouraging messages by noted authors on physical, emotional, mental and spiritual development.

How can Mr. Zee balance intuition and intellect in the start-up process? He feels intuitively that the health clubs are his primary market. But, before spending thousands of dollars marketing all-out to health clubs, he decides to test market in four health clubs in his area. In this way he gathers information (intellect) so his marketing plan is designed to give him and his clients optimum benefits (balancing purpose and profit).

He discovered a critical fact in the test market. Health clubs that emphasized the physical workout and de-emphasized emotional, mental and spiritual aspects of fitness were not productive markets. Health clubs, on the other hand, that did emphasize holistic fitness were excellent "Zeep" markets.

The Zeep Company is forming as a MetaBusiness. A MetaBusiness balances intuition and intellect.

I have come across a high percentage of so-called "purpose" oriented businesses which over-use the intuition. They view the intellect as a culprit to be utilized as little as possible in the decision-making process. In my view, many of these overly idealistic businesses are just as unbalanced and backward as excessively competitive businesses.

In fact, in many ways they are more difficult to deal with than a competitive business. They often give the appearance of caring, sincerity, cooperation, creativity, and honesty, but when it comes time to delivering the goods, they usually fail miserably. A business that runs disproportionately on intuition is not a MetaBusiness.

Mr. Zee followed his intuition balanced with intellect. New information came to light which triggered another intuitive idea. Why not introduce "Zeep" into whole fitness health clubs in Berkeley, Santa Cruz and Boulder?

Again, he balanced intuition with intellect. Rather than install "Zeeps" in all holistic health clubs in the three markets, he researched (intellect) which club was the most respected in each area. He began with one Zeep in each club and waited to see the results.

How to Stop Automatic Thinking

In order for intuition to operate readily you must stop, or at least slow down, automatic thinking. Automatic thinking is intellect at its worst. The mind races out-of-control from one thought to the next. Nine times out of ten automatic thinking leads to more confusion, not more clarity.

What can you specifically do when thinking madly about some business decision whether a problem, difficulty or crisis?

Step 1   Become Aware. Recognize you are in a state of "automatic thinking". Observe the incessant rise and fall of words, images, and thoughts in the mind.

Step 2   Breathe Rhythmically. Take at least three slow rhythmic breaths. Observe your breathing. Place your attention on the breathing process.

Step 3   Activate the Five Senses. Move the focus of your attention away from thinking and toward sensory awareness.

Look around the room. Notice shapes, color, pattern, size, and design. Just look. Do not think, analyze, figure or associate.

Now listen. Hear whatever sounds are now in your immediate environment. A phone rings. A car passes. You clear your throat. A door opens and closes.

Next, touch. Place your attention in your hands, in your fingertips. Feel the textures, the smoothness and roughness of things.

Activate taste and smell. There will be more to experience here at lunch. Consciously taste. Smell the foods cooking.

Step 4   Become Body Conscious. Take a short walk down the block, around the block or in your office building. Walk more slowly. Put your attention into your legs. Feel their alternating movement. Notice the swinging movement of your arms. As you walk you are only a body moving. You are not a mind thinking.

Step 5 Relax. Bring your attention slowly into the back of your neck. Gently roll your neck to the right, then back to the left.

If you are sitting, give your weight up to the chair. Put your attention in your buttocks. Let the chair hold you up. There is no need to grab, cling to your body. Let go in your thighs, hips, legs and lower back. Let the chair do all the work of holding you up.

If you are standing, give your weight up to the floor or ground. Put your attention into your feet. Feel the earth under your feet. Know that the ground will support you. There is no need to grip your muscles. Let go. You will be supported. By giving your weight up to the ground your body will be loose and relaxed.

By letting go of automatic thinking you open up to unexpected possibilities. A hunch, a sudden thought, a powerful feeling, a dream, a creative image... the intuitive process activates in its own playful, non-linear way.

Awaken and Enhance Intuition

Slowing down and stopping automatic thinking will allow intuitive awareness to awaken. Comparing the intuition to a radio, the intellect is the static. When you fine tune the station to its specific frequency, the reception is clear. The intuition comes through.

How can you awaken and enhance intuition?

Step 1 Acknowledge Intuition. Accept openly that there is an awareness process that is not under your control which can assist you in problem solving and decision making.

Step 2 Be Receptive. Listen to unusual thoughts. Pay attention to illogical feelings or emotions. Be open to dream solutions. Be flexible to spontaneous changes in schedules.

Step 3   Break Your Routine. Once in a while do something that breaks your regular routine. Have lunch at a restaurant you would normally never go. Go to a public event you would never attend like a rock concert, a bicycle race or a whistling contest. Take the bus to work instead of driving. Look for opportunities to occasionally change your rigid routine.

Step 4   Create Quiet Time. If possible, on a daily basis create a quiet time of 15-20 minutes. During that time you do something that might be considered by some to be "frivolous".

Shut the door to your office and lie down on the floor. Relax or take a short nap. Read an enjoyable book. Listen to a favorite music tape with headphones. Use the Biocircuits, a relaxation tool described on pages 83-84 of my book *Tuning To The Spiritual Frequencies*. Go into the alpha/theta brain wave state using the Alphatron which induces the relaxed state.

Step 5   Be Playfully Creative. Tap your creative energies. Forget about how good or bad your creation looks, sounds or feels. Finger-print. Sculpt with playdough. Play a harmonica or kazoo. Draw a picture with color crayons. Dance around the house.

Awakening and enhancing intuition is a non-linear process. In other words, you cannot memorize a formula and make it happen whenever you want. In a linear process like intellect, 1 + 1 is always 2. In a non-linear intuitive process 1 + 1 could be most any number except 2.

The unexpected, the spontaneous, the accident, the coincident, and the mistake are events which may present intuitive possibilities. Watch your automatic tendencies to reject and/or deny the unusual. Be willing to see and feel the intuitive information. An unusual occurrence may be presented to you.

Summary of Chapter 7

1. The primary function of the intellect is to separate. In the business world the intellect is used to separate facts and figures.

2. Our educational and economic systems emphasize intellectual development and generally de-emphasize other abilities like intuition, instinct, awareness, creativity, manual dexterity, sensitivity and spirituality.

3. On the positive side the intellect has led us into a technological age which reached its pinnacle with the computer.

4. On the negative side the intellect seems not to know when to stop separating. It tends to hook into dualistic thinking: success / failure, good / bad, right / wrong, win / lose.

5. Learning to separate can be balanced with learning to bring together. Intellectual duality can be balanced with intuitive unity.

6. Once you get into the habit of overusing the intellect, thinking obsessively about your work, you fall into the competitive level.

7. With the information explosion the intellect overloads, short-circuits with the endless current of words, images and concepts. New information means more possibilities, means more choices.

8. On the competitive level you try to "figure out" the best choice. Often this "figuring out" decision-making process leads to confusion.

9. Thinking requires energy. Excessive thinking uses up an unbalanced measure of energy.

10. Getting off the competitive levels onto the creative MetaBusiness levels can be assisted by using intuition in the decision-making process.

11. What is intuition? From one point of view, intuition is awareness of information not immediately available through seeing, hearing, touching, tasting and smelling.

12. Consciously cultivating sensitivity to feelings, flash thoughts and hunches will give you a valuable tool for decision-making in your business or profession.

13. There are overly idealistic businesses which overuse the intuition. They view the intellect as a culprit to be utilized as little as possible in the decision-making process. In my view many of these overly idealistic businesses are just as unbalanced and backward as excessively competitive businesses.

14. A MetaBusiness balances intuition and intellect.

15. In order for intuition to operate readily you must stop, or at least slow down, automatic thinking.

16. Nine times out of ten automatic thinking leads to more confusion not more clarity.

17. You can slow down automatic thinking by:

    1. Becoming Aware
    2. Breathing Rhythmically
    3. Activating the Five Senses
    4. Becoming Body Conscious
    5. Relaxing

18. By letting go of automatic thinking you open up to unexpected possibilities. A hunch, a sudden thought, a powerful feeling, a dream, a creative image... the intuitive process activates in its own playful, non-linear way.

19. You can awaken and enhance intuition by:

    1. Acknowledging Intuition
    2. Being Receptive
    3. Breaking Your Routine
    4. Creating Quiet Time
    5. Being Playfully Creative.

20. In a linear process like intellect, $1 + 1$ is always 2. In a non-linear intuitive process, $1 + 1$ could be most any number except 2.

Chapter 8: The Age of Play

by Michelle Schmidt

We are entering a new age: an age of exploration and fulfillment. No longer is it enough simply to achieve or produce material wealth. *Consciousness* is finally condoned and increasingly exalted by the masses. At last it is "in" to be sensitive to one's planet, one's fellows and even one's self. Cooperation, laughter and fun seem to be replacing competition, seriousness and the work ethic.

We are evolving to a new level of awareness and concern for our spiritual and emotional well-being. We are learning to embrace life and nurture it instead of exploiting it. The question, "What makes *me* happy?" has replaced, "What do others expect of me?" Living in the moment has begun to replace living for retirement.

Living *in the moment* is what kids do best. I am not referring to narcissism but rather to seizing each moment in time and savoring it, really being here *now*. After all, this moment is all we truly have. Yesterday is but a memory and tomorrow has not yet come and perhaps never will. Suddenly, planning for the future takes a second seat to living in today.

Do you ever catch yourself thinking about what you have to do tomorrow, or what life will be like when you have reached a goal? When we are in this state of projection, we are not in the now. As one philosopher said, when you drink tea, drink tea. Don't drink next year's plans!

Children, until we teach them otherwise, have an innate ability to appreciate and participate in the moment. A dust ball or a fallen leaf is a wonderful treasure. Time stands still for them when they play and laugh. There is no worry about who will pay the bills next week or whether their new friend will decide one day to leave them. They are entirely engrossed in the present.

As adults we spend much valuable time trying to imagine the future, as if by predicting events we could somehow protect ourselves from pain and disappointment. In truth we really haven't the power to control other people or our universe to the extent we are often disillusioned into believing. And no amount of planning or fortunetelling, accurate or otherwise, can save us from the hurt and frustration of life's dark moments.

The only thing we can truly control is the way we deal with life. One way is called the Tao: to flow with life and accept life on life's terms. As surfers know, it is impossible to fight the laws of nature such as those governing the waves of the sea. It is far more productive to let go and relax, when caught in a rip tide, than to try and fight this incredible force. These jockeys of the ocean know that if they struggle to reach the surface they will surely drown, but if they let the water go its own course they will eventually pop up to the safety of the surface.

Similarly in life, more often than not, it is futile to fight the process, attempting to control the uncontrollable. It is better to let go and trust the flow, go along for the ride and enjoy the scenery, than to miss the entire journey by trying to make it into something else.

So what does play have to do with all of this? When I speak of play, I am referring to the kinds of funfilled activities that are noncompetitive and oftentimes spontaneous and unplanned. This playfulness is often associated with young children. Childlike play seems to bring us quite quickly to that state of consciousness where time is suspended and the now expands. When in play, there is no future or past, only the present moment. Living in the moment is the only true connection we have with reality. It's all we really ever have, despite what our minds would like us to believe.

Play brings us to a state of bliss and joy that heightens our sensory awareness, lets down our guard, frees up our creativity, releases chemicals that induce rapture, energizes and revitalizes our minds and bodies, and connects us to other people, to our planet and to ourselves. Play is the magic elixir that costs nothing and yet delivers so much fulfillment and pleasure.

Play is food for the soul. It fills the emptiness. It feels like love. It is nurturing and comforting. It is the most natural state I know. It is only because we've been trained culturally not to value play and the resultant feelings, that we have come to forget how to be free and spontaneous.

But all this is changing. The puritan work ethic is slowly being replaced by a more balanced approach to life. It's no longer "hip" to be a workaholic. There are 12-step support groups, books and workshops to help us learn how to bring balance to our lives. Leisure is even encouraged by many companies. "All work and no play makes Johnny a dull boy" is now more than ever a recognized truth.

Companies are realizing that burning people out and replacing them, is far more costly and less productive than caring for their employees. Creative genius and high energy come from balanced periods of work, rest and play. Some companies are even hiring specialists to ensure their employees get the good times they need to remain happy and fulfilled. Happier people are more productive people. And besides, happiness is just a good thing. Attitudes are changing, even in the corporate culture.

So what is play? How do we "do it"? Well, firstly we can take a few pointers from the greatest teachers I know, children. Just watch how children are. Watch what they do. Do what they do and you will begin to experience the joys of play. In my classes and "Funshops" I lead groups in childlike games and activities. I say "I lead" but more accurately the group leads itself, which is the perfect thing. Children, when engaged in spontaneous play, may begin with an idea for their fun but then very quickly that idea melts into a new one. It is a very unstructured, uncalculated flow of events.

The classes and Funshops I facilitate, operate very much the same way. The group has a life of its own and operates very well without the rigid structuring, rules and regulations we as adults are taught we must have in order for things to "work out". In these playtime experiences there are no rules, no expectations, no right or wrong ways to do things, no evaluations, and no competitions.

All events and games are designed to be non-threatening, safe, and validating. So everyone feels like a winner. The environment is one that says "It's OK to be yourself", "It's safe to let down your guard", "No one will ridicule you here", and "You don't have to do anything you don't feel comfortable doing".

Here, there is no pressure to conform or participate. There is no feeling of inadequacy, of not being good enough. Everyone is special and valued, and self-esteem is bolstered to a new level. People start to feel safe enough to take little risks, to be themselves more fully. They begin to step outside of expectations and norms, to a freedom and expansiveness in their thinking and being. They feel more alive, freer, lighter. The armor comes off and an innocent delight takes its place. I see people transformed before my very eyes.

Play is a miracle that has been sorely underrated for too long. I'm glad to see that attitudes are changing. In my Funshops and classes I've had people in their 20's and people in their 70's. There have been school teachers, architects, mothers, students, computer experts, shopkeepers, retirees, and persons in every other occupation you can think of. I see them come alive and find their essence: that pure, unencumbered person that they truly are. I love the bumper sticker that says "It's never too late to have a happy childhood." It's so true.

So why don't we play more? Well for one thing, work has always been valued over play. Words like, "There's no time for play when there's work to be done", "What did you accomplish today?", "Be serious, don't fool around", "Grow up!", "Put away your childish toys and act like an adult" seem to tell us that play is not a valuable use of our time. If it doesn't make money, create status or accomplish some task then it must not be worth doing.

To me that's just pure nonsense. Play is an essential part of life. To be balanced there must be at least an equal amount of play to work. The universe is designed to be a very balanced system. We have dark and light, night and day, up and down, sweet and sour, old and young, and work and play. Not work and more work!

I think we're becoming much more conscious of the necessity to live a balanced life. We've come to realize that we cannot disregard the harmony of nature. Its need to stay in equilibrium is very apparent, and when we forget this we pay a tremendous price. The same is true of ourselves. Without balance we get sick, we die younger than we might, we feel unfulfilled and unhappy. Balance is essential to life.

When I was in therapy, my counselor tried to encourage me to balance my life. She said, "You don't have any trouble being serious and responsible. What you need to practice is lightening up and having some fun! You need to play!" But I didn't know how. I had been practicing being a serious adult for so long, I had forgotten how to really let loose and have fun.

I had to *re-learn* how to play. What I needed was a "Play-Coach": someone who would help me think of ways to have fun; someone who would encourage me to be silly and let go of trying to be perfect; someone who would validate me when I did something playful. But there was no one called a "play coach".

In my late twenties and early thirties I spent a lot of time going to workshops and support groups, reading self-help books, meditating, and exploring the inner depths of my mind and motivations. Days were devoured dealing with pain and grief, digging up old memories, processing them and working through "old stuff", trying to rid myself of the "baggage" of my past. It was all good work and very vital to my evolution as a conscious human being. I like myself better, and as a result, I'm more sensitive to others as well as myself. I'm happier and freer than I've ever been.

Some of the most intense pain accompanied those periods in which I experienced the most significant psychological, emotional, and spiritual growth. I wouldn't trade those times for anything (of course at the time I would have gladly passed!) But amidst the healing pain I realized that I needed to balance my life with joy as well. I searched for workshops and books that could teach me how to get in touch with my joy and playfulness. I found none. If they had been available, I didn't hear about them.

The only place I did find playfulness encouraged and supported was in one particular 12-step support group I attended. There, we practiced getting in touch with our "inner-child" and many playful and childlike activities were suggested and encouraged. But it was still not enough of what I needed.

Finding no alternative, I started my own play groups. I created a class where people could come and explore their childlike selves. A place where joy and spontaneity and autonomy would be encouraged. A place where it would be safe to have fun, to be silly and free. A place where people could gain the tools and the courage to play more in life. Where they would get a chance to balance the pain and seriousness of life with light-hearted laughter and joy.

In these classes and Funshops we throw marshmallows, build forts, play tag, mold playdough, draw with our toes, scream and sing songs, and generally do whatever we please. We play games from our childhood, only *without* the element of competition. We blow bubbles, play on swings, make ice cream sundaes on the floor, and write on the walls with soap crayons. The things you loved to do as a child are the things we do in play class. Sometimes we're outrageous and wild, and sometimes we're quietly content. But always there is a feeling of unrestricted fun and play.

My business partner and friend Greg Nielsen now works with me as a "facilitator of fun". We do corporate Funshops, weekend retreats, and evening play groups, all over the country. Happiness is catching! People *want* to play. I can't imagine doing anything more fulfilling and satisfying for myself than to facilitate the rediscovery and unfoldment of that joyful child within each person who comes to play with us. It was what I needed for *me*, and I love participating in and encouraging joyfulness in others.

I think a new area of specialization is emerging in the human potential movement. In addition to traditional therapists, Play-Coaches are coming: specialists in joy. These people lend encouragement and validation to individuals wishing to explore playfulness and joy. Along with support groups and therapists that deal with problems and pain, there is this other group of facilitators coming on the scene: those who deal with fun and laughter. More and more you will see the emergence of play groups to compliment support groups, and Play-Coaches to compliment psychotherapists. This Age of Play is also the Age of Balance.

What would it be like to visit a "Play-Coach"? The office of a Play-Coach is a place full of light, furnished comfortably, perhaps with large fluffy pillows on a carpeted floor, and appointed with stuffed animals and toys such as yo-yos, bubbles, balls, and balloons, a bowl of popcorn on the table, paper and crayons always within reach. She or he is casually dressed and perhaps wearing animal slippers or colorful, funny socks.

The atmosphere is one of complete safety and there is a feeling of being a peer, an equal with the Play-Coach. The doctor/patient relationship is replaced with a friend/friend, student/student dynamic. The Play-Coach is a facilitator and a validator, rather than an expert or advice giver. The role of the Play-Coach is to encourage individuals to find and *be* themselves, to give validation to whatever they choose to do, and to suggest ideas for fun activities. She or he helps provide a safe environment to explore one's own freedom, spontaneity and playfulness without fear of judgement or rejection.

Perhaps the Play-Coach would meet the person at a park, a swing set, the sand box, a toy store or any other playful place. The Play-Coach might suggest playful activities and exercises that the person could do on their own, and/or the Play-Coach might participate in some of these activities during their time together. They might play games to increase sensory awareness or draw with blindfolds on or with a non-dominant hand. They might build a city with blocks or Leggos or play the Marshmallow Name Game.

The Play-Coach might suggest that the person make a list of those things that used to bring her or him joy as a child, and then encourage her or him to do some of those things now. There would be time for processing, sharing ideas, feelings, barriers and victories. The structure might be completely different each time and could be a weekly get-together, a once-a-month event or a biannual exploration.

Eventually, a person re-learning to play would have no need for the Play-Coach, having developed enough confidence to play on her or his own and having created a network of childful, supportive friends to replace the role that the Play-Coach served in the beginning. The Play-Coach is like training wheels on a bike. They help you get started, and then pretty soon you're ready to ride on your own.

The Play-Coach can be valuable to corporations as well. She or he may be hired to set up playtime experiences for employees at regular intervals. She or he might be requested to design a playfulness program for an entire year, to create a special Funshop for the annual meeting, to hire and train *Joy Committee* personnel, or to develop and implement a playroom facility at the corporate offices.

Corporations are recognizing the need for participating and encouraging the creative process. They can have a vital impact on their employees' productivity and creativity by providing experiences and opportunities for spontaneity and play.

If you think you don't know how to be playful and spontaneous, think back to when you were a child or teenager. Do you remember *planning* to have cookies and milk, or planning to build a fort, or planning to leap up and say "tag, you're it!" to your best friend? And how about cutting class that spring day in the 9th grade. Was *that* in your date book? Life just sort of happened. It was more spontaneous and playful back then.

And it can be again. Start shaking things up today. Do something totally unpredictable. Something you think is unlike you. Dress punk, take a trip on the spur of the moment, rent a convertible and wear a poodle skirt. Anything but the usual. You can't imagine the emotional and physical charge you'll get. Life *can* be exhilarating.

Yes, this is the Age of Play. Get ready to have more fun than you've ever had before! Finally, it's OK to play!

Michelle R. Schmidt, often called "The Play Lady", is a workshop leader, Play-Coach, and writer. Her diverse background in both business and psychology includes work in such fields as the high-tech industry, entertainment, and counseling. She is a native Californian and currently resides in the San Francisco Bay Area. Her book *It's O.K. to Play: An Adult's Guide to Joy and Fulfillment* and the *365 Ways to Playfulness* calendar are scheduled for release in the near future.

Chapter 9: How To Handle A Competitive Business

Similar And Different Businesses

Remember a MetaBusiness stays off the competitive levels and stays on the creative levels. Let's summarize how this is accomplished.

1. Find and manifest your purpose.
2. Balance purpose and profit.
3. Acknowledge that there is a limitless supply in formless substance.
4. Communicate your thoughts to formless substance.
5. Focus on gratitude.
6. Become an energy being.
7. Practice rhythmic alternation.
8. Awaken intuition.
9. Balance intuition and intellect.

As a MetaBusiness stabilized on the creative levels, you will more than likely have to deal with businesses coming from the fearful competitive levels.

There are two broad categories of businesses: businesses that are similar to yours, and businesses that are different from yours.

Generally speaking, you may have more difficulty with businesses that are similar to yours. One reason this may be true is because a competitive business usually identifies that you are in the "same" business. This mistaken identification leads to a fight-or-flight fearful reaction. Their territory is threatened.

Do you recall Mama's Restaurant and Mother's Restaurant in Chapter 3: "Creation Replaces Competition?"

Mama's Restaurant was an established local restaurant. Mother's, a national restaurant chain, moved in across the street.

As long as Betty Johnson, Mama's owner, focused on the "sameness" she was full of anger and fear. As a MetaBusiness leader you must be aware that competitive business leaders will react with anger and fear.

Whatever you are unconscious of controls you. If you are not aware of the fear and anger, there's a tendency to identify with it yourself and temporarily fall back into the competitive levels.

As a MetaBusiness leader, focus on the differences and you will not identify with the "sameness". In the next sections I will give you specific ways to handle negative competitive energies.

You will also have to deal with competitive businesses which are operating in a completely different sphere. They may be suppliers, distributors, retail outlets, subcontractors, etc. They may not perceive you as an immediate threat so it may not be as obvious that they are operating on the competitive levels. Still, you must be aware.

How To Go Into Neutral

Competitive conflicts arise almost daily between businesses. A MetaBusiness leader experiences these emotional tug-of-wars just as any other business person. The difference is that the MetaBusiness person handles the competitive energies by "going into neutral".

What is meant by "going into neutral"? Most people are aware that you can react positively or negatively to any person, place or thing. There is, however, another way of reacting to a competitive threat, choosing not to get caught up into the conflicting territorial fight-or-flight instincts: "going into neutral".

Let me give you a specific example of "going into neutral". A man owned a rental store selling computer and office equipment. His son manufactured an excellent software package which his father carried in the store.

The son sold the software to a mail order business in the same town as his father's store. The father and the creator of the software mail order business knew each other. Every time their paths crossed the father made it clear that he had sole rights to sell his son's software package in that town.

The fellow (John) who operated the mail order business (a MetaBusiness) understood from the manufacturer that this was not true. How did John handle this competitive business situation by going into neutral?

Step 1 Be Aware.

John was conscious of the father's possessive, competitive, fearful feeling. If John had been unaware, he more than likely would have fallen into a competitive conflict with the father.

Step 2 Self-Observation.

John noticed his immediate emotional, mental and verbal reactions. He felt anger and fear tug at his guts. He noticed retaliatory thoughts going through his mind. He chose not to identify with these reactions.

Step 3 Rhythmic Breathing.

John did slow rhythmic breathing through the nose to help him release the negative emotions and "go into neutral".

Step 4 Be Agreeable.

John answered the father in a courteous, friendly voice. He did not put the father on the defensive by saying, "That's not what your son told me." Instead, he said, "I will not sell to the other rental outlets in town, but if people stop by my office asking about it I will sell it to them." John presented a compromising position which the father did not like but could live with.

Step 5 Let Time Pass.

It's amazing how much can be resolved by letting time pass and doing nothing. New possibilities arise. Changes in circumstances resolve the situation. The fearful competitive emotions and thoughts lose their hold on the body and mind.

Letting Go

When you encounter a competitive business that is constantly on the attack, it may be necessary to let go completely. From an energy point of view you may have to use up too much energy handling an antagonistic competitor to the degree that it is no longer worth your while.

As an energy being, it is critical to remember that those around you have an effect on your energies. Competitors that are ruthless, manipulative, cut-throat, lying, and cheating put out a powerful negative energy. Interacting with them on any level gives them energy.

By completely letting go of a connection with a ruthless competitor you do not give them any time, attention or energy. On an energy level they now have less power. Your MetaBusiness is one less business that will interact with them.

Obviously, letting go is easy to say but not necessarily easy to do. Letting go may mean your profits will decrease for a time. You have to be willing to face your fears head on. Remember, when you focus on the limitless supply in formless substance, there are limitless opportunities. A new situation will arise which will be much better.

If you find yourself concretized in fear, you might use the following releasing exercise. It is called "Touch and Let Go".

Write down keywords that describe the fear. For example, "Fear of financial losses when I stop dealing with the competitive company." Sit comfortably at a table or desk and place the sheet of paper in front of you. Next, press the fingers of both hands firmly over the keywords. Touch for a second or two, then let go for a second or two.

Repeat this touch and let go process rhythmically for about 10-20 minutes. At the end of the session rip the paper up and throw it away. It's advisable to rest about a half hour before resuming your regular schedule. This gives the psyche an opportunity to get used to the new feeling of not being afraid.

Letting go is a strategic option when operating a MetaBusiness. Letting go may mean short-term losses. On the other hand, it strengthens a MetaBusiness' purpose.

Once a business gets in the habit of compromising purpose for profit, it entrenches itself in the fearful competitive frequencies. Sometimes handling a competitive business means letting go and not dealing with them at all.

Vigilant Awareness

The competitive forces run rampant. Almost every institution from educational to medical is, at its core, competitive. It appears to be "normal" since it is woven into the very fabric of our society.

Staying on the creative levels requires Vigilant Awareness. You must be on the look out. The competitive energies can trigger off at any time. The "competitive spirit" programmed into your subconscious can be activated in less than a second.

Vigilant Awareness means choosing to be eternally watchful. You see clearly that few are on the creative levels, many are on the competitive levels. As a MetaBusiness person you especially have to be vigilantly aware of competitive business leaders.

What are some of the signs to look for that warn you of competitive activities?

Verbal attacks often signal a competitive motivation. The direct verbal attack to your face is obviously competitive. It is designed to put you into the fight-or-flight automatic reaction. A competitive person likes to deal with another competitive person.

In many ways indirect verbal attacks can be more insidious. You may hear through the grapevine that such and such a competitive company is going to hire your top salespeople. You wonder. Is it true? Is it just a rumor? You worry. You're afraid. You're momentarily on the competitive level.

Notice sudden nonverbal behaviors that are out of character. When a competitive type feels threatened (territorial instinct), she or he retreats in order to plan her or his next attack.

Being vigilantly aware, you will notice the usual communications have slowed to a trickle or stopped altogether. Prepare yourself for the return. Anchor yourself in your creative center and stay in neutral.

Often a competitive type instinctively feels the energizing effect of your creative energies. She or he wants to be around you. She or he wants to dump her or his emotional problems on you.

Giving a sympathetic ear can tune you into the competitive frequencies. Suddenly you feel your energies being drained. You have to go and the person will not stop talking. You speak. They do not hear what you're saying.

Be vigilantly aware. This fearful competitive type will mesmerize you with their verbal barrage and then spring something on you. Watch out. It may not be wise to say yes or no right away.

Remember, as a vigilantly aware MetaBusiness leader, a competitive person is not "good" or "bad". Her or his behavior follows logically from her or his belief. If you fall into the dualistic thought pattern that you are "right" and she or he is "wrong", then you attune yourself, even temporarily, to the competitive frequencies.

Act and Speak Impersonally

Often fearful, competitive persons act and speak on a personal level. They may ask, for example, where you grew up or what neighborhood you live in shortly after meeting you. They start asking personal questions before any sort of genuine friendship has evolved.

On the other hand, they may offer all sorts of personal information about themselves without your asking. They may talk about problems with spouse or children. Perhaps they give a run-down on their life history.

Besides speaking on a personal level, they may act on a personal level. Perhaps they give an inappropriate gift. A competitive business person may use her or his power to impress or gain advantage over you.

Remember, whether they are conscious of it or not, competitive persons will act and speak on a personal level in order to manipulate, use and "set you up for the kill". All the personal charms and wiles are ploys designed to bring you into the competitive levels and out of the creative levels.

As a MetaBusiness person, you can remain firm yet flexible in your creative center by acting and speaking impersonally in all your business dealings, especially with highly competitive types.

If you are asked personal questions that have no bearing on the business dealings at hand, you do not have to answer. There is no need to go on the defensive. Simply go into neutral and change the course of the conversation back to a courteous impersonal exchange.

Persistence here is a must. A competitive type may not be used to interacting with a creative MetaBusiness person. The "successful" high-powered competitor may be used to controlling the situation. Usually they will persist in their approach. They may try every tactic that has worked for them in the past.

Conscious persistence is a more potent force than unconscious persistence. Continue to act and speak with friendly impersonality. Eventually, they will adjust, though with discomfort, to your approach. Or, if it's just too uncomfortable, you may discover they want no dealings with you whatsoever. In that case, they may be doing you a favor.

Whenever possible avoid business activities, especially with highly competitive types, when you are tired, emotionally upset, sick, drained or thinking excessively about personal problems. You are better off cancelling these meetings until you return to an impersonal stance. Most competitive types will instinctively exploit a weakness.

Staying On the Creative Level

Handling a competitive business and handling competitive people require that you stay on the creative levels. How do you know you're on the creative levels? Let's review once again:

1. You are motivated from purpose not profit.

2. You balance purpose and profit.

3. You are cooperative rather than combative.

4. You acknowledge your competitive fears.

5. You have faith in the creative process.

6. You are innovating not stagnating.

7. You are grateful every day.

8. You enjoy a holistic lifestyle.

9. You flow with your life rhythms.

10. You respond to intuitive thoughts and feelings.

11. You balance intuition and intellect.

12. You let go and neutralize your fears.

Now reread each of the twelve indicators above. With all honesty rate yourself on a 0-10 scale; ten is the highest rating and zero is the least.

A rating of 6 or below suggests it may be wise for you to take action to restore balance. For example, if you are not acknowledging your competitive fears, chances are you are unconscious of them or avoiding them. Remember, whatever you are unconscious of tends to control you.

Unconscious lack feelings mean you have a fear of not having enough. Your unconsciousness will more or less guarantee continued lack. Notice the exact moment when you think and feel the opportunities and supply are limited. Acknowledge your fear and begin the letting-go process.

Handling competitive people demands that you first and foremost learn to handle your own competitive tendencies. You will find it much easier to handle the competitive energies in others if you are well on your way to mastering the competitive energies you have a habit of identifying with.

Staying on the creative levels is a way of life not a short-term gimmick. To stabilize on the creative level requires a lifetime commitment. It may take several generations for the creative way of doing business to be more common than the competitive way.

It's a waste of time and energy to worry about when the business world will change. Start with you. Do what you can do each day to stabilize and maintain yourself on creative levels. The world is the way it is. Focusing excessively on what's wrong and complaining only feeds more energy into the competitive system.

Summary of Chapter 9

1. There are two broad categories of business: (1) businesses that are similar to yours, and (2) businesses that are different from yours.

2. You may have more difficulties with similar businesses because often a competitive business identifies that you are in the same business.

3. This mistaken identification leads to a fight-or-flight fearful reaction. Their territory is threatened.

4. Whatever you are unconscious of controls you. If you are not aware of the fear and anger, there's a tendency to identify with it yourself and temporarily fall back into the competitive levels.

5. A MetaBusiness person handles the competitive energies by "going into neutral".

6. The steps to going into neutral are: 1. Be aware, 2. Self-observation, 3. Rhythmic breathing, 4. Be agreeable and 5. Let time pass.

7. When you encounter a competitive business that is constantly on the attack, it may be necessary to let go completely.

8. As an energy being it is critical to remember that those around you have an effect on your energies. Competitors that are ruthless, manipulative, cutthroat, lying, and cheating put out a powerful negative energy. Interacting with them on any level gives them energy.

9. By completely letting go of a connection with a ruthless competitor you do not give them any time, attention or energy. They now have less power.

10. If you find yourself concretized in fear, you might want to do a "Touch And Let Go".

11. Staying on the creative levels requires Vigilant Awareness. You must be on the look out. The competitive energies can trigger off at any time.

12. What are some of the signs of competitive behavior? Watch for: 1. Direct verbal attacks; 2. Indirect verbal attacks; 3. Unexpected retreats; 4. Sudden appearances; and 5. Dumping emotional problems.

13. Remember, as a vigilantly aware MetaBusiness leader a competitive person is not "good" or "bad". Her or his behavior follows logically from her or his belief.

14. If you fall into the dualistic thought pattern that you are "right" and they are "wrong", then you attune yourself, even temporarily, to the competitive frequencies.

15. Often a fearful, competitive type acts and speaks on a personal level.

16. A competitive type acts and speaks on a personal level in order to manipulate, use and "set you up for the kill".

17. All the personal charms and wiles are ploys designed to bring you into the competitive levels and out of the creative levels.

18. As a MetaBusiness person you can remain firm yet flexible in your creative center by acting and speaking impersonally in all your business dealings, especially with highly competitive types.

19. Whenever possible avoid business activities when you are tired, emotionally upset, sick, drained or thinking excessively about personal problems.

20. Handling competitive people demands that you first and foremost learn to handle your own competitive tendencies.

21. Staying on the creative levels is a way of life not a short-term gimmick or the latest fad. To stabilize on the creative level is a lifetime commitment.

22. It's a waste of time and energy to worry about when the business world will change. Start with you. Do what you can do each day.

Chapter 10: Money Buys Free Time

Money

I highly recommend a book titled *Science And Sanity* by Alfred Korzybski. He focuses on what he calls semantic reactions. Semantic reactions are the automatic mental-emotional-physical responses we have to words.

As a MetaBusiness person, it is wise to become aware of your semantic reaction to the word *money*. Money... what do you feel? Can you feel your automatic semantic reaction?

Be conscious. Observe your immediate response. Money... Money... Money... Money... Money... Money... Money. Do you feel the emotional charge the word money carries?

Having money, not having money... Making a lot of money, spending a lot of money... working hard for money. Never having enough money... borrowing money, paying back money. It's amazing how much time and energy we "spend" focusing on money. No wonder so many emotional semantic reactions are activated just by saying the word money.

Take out a dollar. Look at it and touch it consciously. What is it in the physical sense? It's paper. Review the process of how paper money is created from seed to tree to paper to printing.

Now take out a coin. Look at it and touch it consciously. What is it in the physical sense? It's metal. Review the process of how metal money is created from minerals to mining to smelting to casting.

Continue touching, looking, being sensory aware of the dollar and coin. The paper and metal are made up of atoms, dynamic whirling patterns of energy. Atoms are energy structures built up from electrons, protons and neutrons.

A physicist, a chemist and biologist could get together and write several volumes on the scientific data known about paper and metal. Reading about the physical properties of money would probably put most of us to sleep. It certainly would introduce a new set of semantic reactions associated with money.

Take a short break from reading this chapter. Touch the dollar and the coin. Put your attention in your fingertips as you touch. Say out loud, "This dollar and this coin are patterns of energy in a dynamic energy world".

Now touch the other things around you like the chair, the table, your clothes and say, "This is a pattern of energy in a dynamic energy world". Has your semantic reaction to the word money changed?

Time

> *"Time is the inexplicable raw material of everything. With it all is possible; without it, nothing. The supply of time is truly a daily miracle, an affair genuinely astonishing, when we examine it. You wake up in the morning, and Lo! Your purse is magically filled with twenty-four hours of the unmanufactured time of the universe! It is yours. It is the most precious of possessions."*

Arnold Bennett, from his book *How To Live 24 Hours A Day*.

There are fundamentally two types of time: (1) clock time and (2) psychological time. Clock time is the measurement of time in hours, minutes, seconds, etc. Psychological time is the feelings we experience of time going quickly or slowly.

A competitive business often "buys into" the belief that "time is money". They misuse clock time by not recognizing and allowing the experience of psychological time.

A large midwest tractor manufacturer hired a new production manager to increase worker efficiency and save the company money. He instituted a new company policy. Everyone had to punch out when they went to the bathroom, and punch back in when they returned.

The plan backfired. It immediately decreased production and lost the company money. The workers were so outraged by the bathroom time clock that they slowed down the work pace.

The production manager began firing. The workers retaliated with a strike. Fortunately, the president of the company intervened. He eliminated the bathroom time clock and fired the production manager.

A MetaBusiness leader understands the value of psychological time. If employees feel time dragging by, why not encourage them to change that feeling. Perhaps they need a short break. Maybe they could go to the Energy Room to recharge their life force.

The Energy Room is the room I mentioned in earlier chapters where there are energy tools like alphatrons, relaxation circuits, multi-wave oscillators, hemi-sync music tapes, metaforms, crystals, color lamps, etc.

A MetaBusiness creates an environment where clock time and psychological time can interact harmoniously. As a result, an ever-changing dynamic balance manifests between clock and psychological time. Experiencing free time usually leads to wiser use of clock time.

Cash Balanced With Credit

There are essentially two kinds of money (1) cash and (2) credit. Cash is the actual amount of money you have at your disposal at any given time. Credit is the money you have at your disposal that you borrow. Credit is money you have not earned yet. With credit you pay to use someone else's cash.

What happens when there is too much cash or too much credit? A business falls to the competitive levels activating the dualistic fight-or-flight instincts.

When a business stores up too much cash, the creative power that money symbolizes is not utilized. The excessive storing of cash indicates a feast-or-famine reaction which is based in fear. The law of the pendulum (opposites) works in extremes on the competitive levels. The hording of cash (gold, silver) leads inevitably to cash flow problems.

With little or no cash flow a competitive business person is often afraid of losing everything. The survival instinct kicks in; she or he stalks credit. The tendency is to over-extend her or his debt obligations, but then the cash flow is not strong enough to balance the debts.

Remaining firmly on the creative levels reduces drastically the intensity of fear.

Lowering the intensity and shortening the duration of fear allows for greater clarity and flexibility. A dynamic balance between cash and credit, which is specific to your business, comes out of awareness on the creative level.

There are no fixed formulas for cash/credit equilibrium. And, in fact, strict adherence or belief in a magic formula is an indication of competitive fear. Every day is different, every situation is different, every business opportunity is different. Centered on the creative levels, you will see the wisdom of the specific proportion between cash and credit with each opportunity that arises.

A fearful competitive economic system compulsively pushes credit, more credit and even more credit. The "buy now, pay later" mentality eventually leads to its opposite, "pay now, buy later". In some parts of the world, even now, the consequences of the "pay now, buy later" reaction to "buy now, pay later" means no money for food, much less clothing and shelter.

Famine, starvation, death and disease are directly related to feasting, gluttony, excess living and short-sighted health measures. Those on the competitive levels will see the relationship between the two as a threat to profits. Those on the creative levels will see the relationship as strengthening their resolve to balance cash/credit and purpose/profit.

Recycling Profits

When a person is living on the competitive levels, profits often trigger a desire to buy more things. As the profits increase, the successful winner feeling leads to the failure loser feeling. Competitive types must display their success by purchasing in excess.

In and of itself there's nothing wrong with buying things. What can be a difficulty is the competitive motivation for buying things that are not needed or required. The more profits are compulsively spent to show-off success, the greater the fear of failure.

The MetaBusiness person remains on the creative levels by continually monitoring the balance between purpose and profits. The MetaBusiness person clearly realizes that in order to nurture purpose an appropriate proportion of profits must be recycled into the growing MetaBusiness.

Remember, in a MetaBusiness the purpose motive replaces the profit motive. Competitive individuals, competitive companies that make profits the bottom line without acknowledging and nurturing purpose will usually, sooner or later, have cash flow problems.

There will be a compulsion to spend the profits unwisely. The profit motive is based on the fight/flight fear instinct. It is common knowledge among psychological counselors that fear-based decisions are often unwise.

When you recycle profits in a MetaBusiness you put significant value on the purpose motive. In order for the businesses' purpose to be strong, dynamic and ever-unfolding, profits must be recycled wisely and proportionately.

A MetaBusiness does not operate from fear so there is no need to waste valuable nurturing money on showing-off or puffing-up the chest with animal dominance. If there is genuine purpose in spending profits for a new sign, building, phone system, etc., then the profits are recycled wisely to nurture purpose.

Staying solidly on the creative levels requires vigilant attention to purpose motivated recycling of profits. Extravagant expenditures on unneeded things or services usually indicates a competitive profit-motivated individual/business. Review how you spend your profits. Can you clearly see your motivation? Do you recycle profits to nurture and strengthen purpose?

Consumerism

By "consumerism" I mean the belief, promotion and practice of buying what is not needed. Consumerism is the creed and dogma of the competition cult. The more a consumer buys, whether it is needed or not, the more a competitive business profits.

The competitive economic system with its fear-centered decision makers, which include politicians, lawyers, bankers, corporate leaders, lobbyists, etc., have made it all too easy for consumers to buy what they do not need. Easy credit does not encourage people to make wise and needed purchases. Consumer advertising uses brainwashing techniques, repeating messages millions of times until an artificial need is created.

If you're in a business which creates an artificial need to buy what is not needed, you are in a competitive business. If you have a sincere desire to get off the competitive levels, you may want to begin the process of recycling your profits into services and products that fill a genuine, heartfelt need.

One of the most blatant forms of consumerism is the fad. A mass hysteria sweeps through the marketplace. Everyone has to have one. If you don't have one, you're just not with it.

Fad consumerism is especially prevalent in the children's toy market. Some years ago the cabbage patch doll craze had adults spending hundreds of dollars above the retail price. Their kid had to have one, and they would do most anything to get one. Recently, I have seen used cabbage patch dolls in thrift stores for a dollar or two.

A MetaBusiness identifies genuine needs, then creates products and/or services that fulfill those needs. There is a growing need today for organic, pesticide-free produce. As individuals become more health conscious, organic produce will continue to generate greater profits.

There is also a genuine need today for alternative education systems. As purposeful MetaBusinesses identify the need and create productive educational alternatives based on cooperation and creativity, competitive educational systems will begin to diminish in dominance.

Spending money exclusively for what you do not need is unbalanced addictive behavior. A business that intentionally promotes and advertises to entice addicts and shopaholics to "buy... buy... buy" will eventually plummet into "failure".

Money Buys Free Time

An individual with a creative MetaBusiness, values free time over and above anything. In fact, they see that money buys free time. Free time gives the opportunity to pursue and enjoy creativity, learning, spiritual practices, renewal and just "doing nothing".

One of the wisest ways for a MetaBusiness to recycle its profits is by giving its leaders and co-creator employees more free time to enjoy living life. Driving people to work harder and longer, burns them out until they get sick, quit or get fired. On the competitive level people are disposable. You can always shop for a new employee like you can for groceries.

The founder of the Patagonia Sporting Wear Company buys free time, about eight months a year, to pursue his love of the outdoors - rock climbing and fishing. Patagonia's employees are encouraged to pursue their interests as well.

Today with the international communication systems, a MetaBusiness leader can buy free time to enjoy what they love to do most and still be just a phone call, satellite page, next day mail, fax or computer screen away from their business.

Every year more and more business leaders are discovering that free time away from the business can improve, enhance and increase purpose and profits.

Computer and communication technology allows MetaBusiness leaders to create home offices. This gives them the freedom to spontaneously take off a day or part of a day and still complete necessary tasks. Balancing work time with free time increases creativity, innovation, energy and purpose.

Compulsive competitive types usually have great difficulty buying free time to do what they want to do. Often there is a fear that everything will fall apart if they are not "staying on top of things". Guilt is mixed in with fear, blocking them from ever truly enjoying the fruits of their labor.

A MetaBusiness person knows when to rest, relax, rejuvenate, regenerate and renew. She or he realizes that there is a dynamic balance between work time and free time. Working too much stagnates a growing business. On the other hand, playing too much leads to neglect and malnourishes the MetaBusiness.

Spending money on free time while letting go of fear and guilt will benefit a MetaBusiness in ways that cannot be predicted.

Summary of Chapter 10

1. As a MetaBusiness person, it is wise to become aware of your semantic reaction to the word *money*.

2. Take out a dollar and a coin. Touch them. Put your attention in your fingertips as you touch. Say out loud, "This dollar and this coin are patterns of energy in a dynamic energy world".

3. There are two types of time: 1) clock time and 2) psychological time. Clock time is the measurement of time in hours, minutes, seconds, etc. Psychological time is the feelings we experience of time going quickly or slowly.

4. A competitive business often "buys into" the belief that "time Is money". They misuse clock time by not recognizing and allowing the experience of psychological time.

5. A MetaBusiness leader understands the value of psychological time. If an employee (co-creator) feels time dragging by why not encourage her or him to change that feeling. Perhaps she or he needs a short break. Maybe she or he could go to the Energy Room to recharge her or his life force.

6. The Energy Room is a room where there are energy tools like alphatrons, relaxation circuits, multi-wave oscillators, hemi-sync music tapes, metaforms, crystals, color lamps, etc.

7. A MetaBusiness balances cash with credit. What usually happens when there is too much cash or too much credit? A business falls to the competitive level activating the dualistic fight-or-flight instincts.

8. There are no fixed formulas for cash/credit balance. And, in fact, strict adherence or belief in a magic formula is an indicator of competitive fear.

9. Every day is different, every situation is different, every business opportunity is different. Centered on the creative level, you will see the wisdom of the specific proportion between cash and credit with each opportunity that arises.

10. When a person is on the competitive levels, profits often trigger a desire to buy more things. Competitive types must display their success by purchasing in excess.

11. The MetaBusiness person clearly realizes that in order to nurture purpose an appropriate proportion of profits must be recycled into the growing MetaBusiness.

12. "Consumerism" is the belief, promotion and practice of buying what is not needed.

13. The competitive economic system with its fear-centered decision makers have made it all too easy for consumers to buy what they do not need.

14. Consumer advertising uses brainwashing techniques, repeating messages millions of times until an artificial need is created.

15. One of the most blatant forms of consumerism is the fad. A mass hysteria sweeps through the marketplace. Everyone has to have one. If you don't have one, you're just not with it.

16. A MetaBusiness identifies genuine needs, then creates products and/or services that fulfill those needs.

17. An individual with a creative MetaBusiness values free time over and above anything. In fact, they see that money buys free time. Free time gives the opportunity to pursue and enjoy creativity, learning, spiritual practices, renewal and just "doing nothing".

18. One of the wisest ways for a MetaBusiness to recycle its profits is by giving its leaders and co-creator employees more free time to enjoy living life.

19. Driving people to work harder and longer burns them out until they get sick, quit or get fired. On the competitive level people are disposable. You can always shop for a new employee like you can for groceries.

20. Today with the international communication systems, a MetaBusiness leader can buy free time to enjoy what they love to do most and still be just a phone call, satellite page, next day mail, fax, computer screen, etc., away from their business.

21. Compulsive competitive types usually have great difficulty buying free time to do what they want to do. Often there is a fear that everything will fall apart if they are not "staying on top of things". Guilt is mixed with fear, blocking them from ever truly enjoying the fruits of their labor.

22. A MetaBusiness person knows when to rest, relax, rejuvenate, regenerate and renew. She or he realizes that there is a dynamic balance between work time and free time. Working too much stagnates a growing business. On the other hand, playing too much leads to neglect and malnourishes the growing business.

Chapter 11: MetaBusiness Advertising

Adult Infantilism

MetaBusiness advertising presents a clear, accurate, factual soft-sell. Competitive advertising hits hypnotically with a confusing, inaccurate, half-truth hard-sell. A competitive business appeals to infantile adult behaviors. They advertise their products/services by purposely triggering compulsions, addictions, habits, obsessions, and fears.

As more and more individuals outgrow the fearful competitive levels, they will mature emotionally. MetaBusiness advertising agencies will emerge to serve MetaBusinesses on creative levels. Manipulative advertising techniques will not be effective with these non-competitive, creative individuals.

In the meantime, adult infantilism is rampant. What are some of the behaviors of an infantile adult? Here is a partial list:

- Intense likes and dislikes
- Emotions influence actions
- Changeable moods
- Weak judgement
- Suggestive
- Emotional outbreaks
- Copies others readily
- Exaggerates
- Lacks discrimination and evaluation
- Prejudiced
- Sexual immaturity
- Easily intimidated

Gradually, there will be more and more mature, creative-level adults who will be turned off by competitive advertising and responsive to MetaBusiness advertising.

What are some of the behaviors of a mature adult? Here is a partial list:

- Moderate likes and dislikes
- Thinking and senses influence actions
- Emotional stability
- Makes wise decisions
- Gathers the facts
- Reserves judgement
- Understanding
- Sexual maturity
- Deals with fears effectively
- Well-developed intuition
- Makes accurate statements
- Learns from mistakes
- Power of concentration
- Healthy relationships

General Semantics

I recommend every MetaBusiness co-creator learn General Semantics and apply it to every phase of business especially advertising. General Semantics was first introduced as a system by Alfred Korzybski in 1933. He wrote a book, *Science and Sanity*, which advocated that we apply the methods of science to the way we use symbols, images, words, etc.

When we create a map that accurately reflects the actual territory, we can travel from point A to point B without difficulty. An inaccurate map, on the other hand, misleads, confuses, angers, frustrates, etc. You cannot get from point A to point B.

MetaBusiness advertising creates ads that accurately portray the products and services. To the best of their ability the MetaBusiness co-creators use words and images that reflect the products and services "truthfully", "honestly", "precisely" and "accurately". This effort is felt by the prospective buyers. They sense the sincerity, clarity and purpose. When they check out the products and services, they are not disappointed. They do not feel lied to.

Often, in a competitive business, the bottom line is profit. Competitive advertising will produce advertising using words and images which do not accurately represent the products and services.

Instead, they show and tell the buyer what will get them to buy. Manipulation, lies, misrepresentations, half-truths, omissions are used to stimulate spending.

The competition in the food industry had companies making wild, unsubstantiated claims in their advertising and on their packaging. The U.S. Food and Drug Administration now tests claims in the laboratory.

One nutritional weight-loss food manufacturer was ordered to take its popular diet cookie off the market. The package advertising claimed it was low in calories, fat and cholesterol. An independent lab analysis revealed the cookie had twice the calories, nearly double the fat content, and was substantially higher in cholesterol than claimed.

Training in General Semantics will assist MetaBusiness co-creators in consciously creating advertisements which use the accurate information at that time. It is critical. Whether inadvertent or blatant, the weight-loss food manufacturer was dealt a near fatal blow. It's good business to practice MetaBusiness advertising.

Semantic Reactions

A semantic reaction is an automatic, mechanical, habitual response to a person, place, thing, sign, symbol, image, word, etc. Infantile adults are, for the most part, relatively unconscious of their semantic reactions. Competitive advertisers can be masters at triggering semantic reactions in order to get a sale.

Competitive advertisers want you to identify with their products and services. There is nothing wrong with that in and of itself. Where competitive advertising "goes wrong" is when it gets potential buyers to identify by purposely triggering infantile likes and dislikes which often have nothing to do with the product or service.

Recall the old cigarette ads. You'll be a "real man" if you smoke a particular cigarette brand. You'll be a "sexy" woman if you smoke another brand. These infantile semantic reactions brought millions to their death bed.

When you are conscious of your semantic reactions, there are choices. You can choose to identify, not identify, wait and see, etc. MetaBusiness advertising encourages awareness, consciousness, choices and free will. Competitive advertising discourages these mature adult traits.

Competitive advertisers, competitive businesses often do extensive market research and test marketing to find out what automatic semantic reactions to activate. Copywriters and commercial artists take this information and create words and images that stimulate intense semantic reactions. People have to buy.

MetaBusinesses would be wise to hire copywriters and commercial artists who are trained in General Semantics. Being aware of semantic reactions and the power to unleash megavolts of human energy implies responsible use of words and images.

MetaBusiness decision makers would be wise to train thoroughly in General Semantics. A semantic sensitivity will develop into a semantic sense. As a result, words and images used to communicate your MetaBusiness products and services would be selected carefully and consciously.

When creating and reviewing your advertising, take care not to use coercion, lies, half-truths, appeals to infantile compulsions, false urgency, etc. Instead, focus on choice, free will, awareness, quality of life, plenty of time, clarity, accuracy, etc. You will attract customers on the creative level who will recognize and appreciate your semantic sensitivity.

The Ad Is Not The Product

The ad is not the product. This statement seems obvious enough. All too often, though, the advertisement creators and the potential buyers who see and hear the advertisement unconsciously identify the ad and the product. In fact, you cannot drive the picture of a car. You cannot eat the hamburger in a television commercial,

Alfred Korzybski introduced into General Semantics the "consciousness of abstracting" in order to remember the difference between the nonverbal, non-picture level and the verbal/picture level. When you are conscious of abstracting, you know you are aware of some characteristics of the event, person, place or thing and are not aware of most of the characteristics. Any advertisement presents a limited view of a product or service.

Naturally, a business uses advertising to communicate to potential buyers the advantages of purchasing a product or service. A competitive business advertiser generally is not conscious of the "orders of abstractions". They tend to confuse the "orders of abstraction" unconsciously believing everything presented in the ad is the product. In extreme cases they may believe everything has been presented.

What are the "orders of abstractions" as given in General Semantics? The silent, energy level product is always totally nonverbal. No matter what you say about it you cannot say all about anything.

The first order abstraction is the picture we form in our mind. When we listen or see an ad we abstract from an abstraction -- we form a picture from a picture. The advertisement creators abstract a few, usually the best, characteristics, and then the potential customers abstract a few points from the ad.

Do you see how removed a customer is from an actual nonverbal experience of the product or service? The customer does not have an experience of the product. They have an experience of the ad. The ad is not the product.

The second order abstraction is what we say about our experience of the ad which is even further removed from an actual non-verbal sensory-level experience. Then, what we say about what we said and what someone else says about what we said is a third order abstraction, etc.

As a MetaBusiness advertiser trained in General Semantics, it is a top priority that your ads represent the nonverbal product as clearly and precisely as possible. When a customer experiences your ad and then experiences your product, you want them to be similar in quality. Contradictory experiences will alienate customers, especially customers who are conscious and on the creative level.

MetaBusiness Advertising Tools

There are five General Semantics tools which will assist you in creating a MetaBusiness ad. You may not specifically use them in the ad. Keeping them in mind, however, during the creative process will guide you out of the competitive levels. The five tools are:

1. Indexing

2. Dating

3. Etc.

4. Quotes

5. Hyphens

Indexing

Let's call your product or service x. When you consciously index, you remember that x_1 is not x_2 is not x_3. If you manufacture pencils you must remember every pencil is different even though they may appear to look the same. Indexing will help you to be more flexible. When an occasional customer complains about pencil x_n, you will respond less defensively. You will want to examine pencil x_n to see if it does have a defect.

Dating

Pencil x_1 1990 is not the same as pencil x_1 1985 the day it was manufactured. As a MetaBusiness you must be conscious of how your product or service changes in time. Dating is required in the food and drug businesses. When you create your ad, keep dating in mind.

Etc.

Etcetera means "and so forth and so on". Whatever you say and show in your pencil ad you can never say and show everything about the pencil. Once you have completed your ad, remember to put an etc. after it in your mind. This keeps your mind open and on the creative levels. Believing you have said everything about the pencil in your advertisement will close your mind keeping you on the competitive level.

Quotes

Using "quotes" around a word is a reminder that the word may be "loaded". In other words, customers may have a semantic reaction which creates confusion, negativity, misunderstanding, etc. In the copywriting phase of your MetaBusiness ad you may want to put "quotes" around many of the words then take time to reflect on the possible semantic reactions of your customers. If the meaning of a word is unclear, you want to clarify what you mean or use a different word.

Hyphens

In General Semantics a hyphen is used between words to indicate connections. Thoughts and feelings, for example, are not totally separate. Thoughts-feelings are interconnected. Body-mind are connected.

MetaBusiness Ads

What makes an advertisement a MetaBusiness ad? The quality of energy used to create the ad is of prime importance. Competitive advertising is based on fear. MetaBusiness advertising is based on the freedom to choose.

Next in importance are quality of words, images and sounds used in creating the MetaBusiness ad. Words, images and sounds which trigger competition, fear, compulsion, rush, antagonism, anger, etc., may indicate an ad on the competitive level.

All too often the words lowest, most, least, best, first, tallest, longest, shortest, complete, largest, etc., are overused and misused. Implying you are better than, tends to be a competitive, fear-based approach to advertising. Avoid these types of words when possible.

Another tendency of competitive advertising is to say too much in too small a space in display advertising, or too short a time in radio/TV advertising.

In MetaBusiness advertising you will often say and show less to communicate more. This will often generate a quality feeling about the quality of the product/service. Unfortunately, many Metabusinesses have not learned how to create advertisements which emanate a creative level energy.

All too often old competitive advertising methods are used which misrepresent the products and services. Usually this is unintentional and happens because of a lack of know-how.

I heard a 30-second MetaBusiness radio commercial that went as follows. A Tibetan bell was struck firmly. The reverberation continued for 25 seconds. You felt peaceful, quiet and meditative. Then a soft, non-intrusive male voice said, "Visit the Peaceful Music Store at 15th and Broadway."

A display ad in the New Age Telephone Book of Southern California impressed me as an example of a MetaBusiness ad. In a 7 1/2" x 4 1/2" space there were few words with large letters. "A New Age Resource Center - The Transformation. Featuring unique, enlightening and regenerative items." These easy to read lines were followed by the number and address.

As a MetaBusiness you want your ads to accurately reflect the products and services. Use the tools of General Semantics as well as some of the tips presented in this chapter to assist you in creating MetaBusiness ads.

Summary of Chapter 11

1. MetaBusiness advertising presents a clear, accurate, factual, soft-sell. Competitive advertising hits hypnotically with a confusing, inaccurate, half-truth, hard-sell.

2. A competitive business appeals to infantile adult behaviors. They advertise their products/services by purposely triggering compulsions, addictions, habits, obsessions, fears, etc.

3. Gradually, there will be more and more mature, creative-level adults who will be turned off by competitive advertising and responsive to MetaBusiness advertising.

4. A MetaBusiness co-creator would be wise to learn and apply General Semantics to every phase of business, especially advertising. General Semantics uses the methods of science to the way we use symbols, images, and words.

5. MetaBusiness advertising creates ads that accurately portray the products and services to the best of their ability at that time.

6. A semantic reaction is an automatic, mechanical, habitual response to a person, place, thing, sign, symbol, image, word, etc. Infantile adults are, for the most part, relatively unconscious of their semantic reactions. Competitive advertisers can be masters at triggering semantic reactions in order to get a sale.

7. Where competitive advertising "goes wrong" is when it gets potential buyers to identify by purposely triggering infantile likes and dislikes which often have nothing to do with the product or service.

8. When you are conscious of your semantic reactions, there are choices. You can choose to identify, not identify, wait and see, etc. MetaBusiness advertising encourages awareness, consciousness, choices and free will.

9. The ad is not the product. In fact, you cannot drive the picture of a car - you cannot eat the hamburger in a television commercial.

10. When you are conscious, you know you are aware of some characteristics of the event, person, place or thing and are not aware of most of the characteristics. Any advertisement presents a very limited view of a product or service.

11. The customer is removed from an actual nonverbal experience of the product. The customer does not have an experience of the product. They have an experience of the ad. The ad is not the product.

12. As a MetaBusiness advertiser trained in General Semantics, it is a top priority that your ads represent the nonverbal product as clearly and precisely as possible. Contradictory experiences will alienate customers, especially customers who are conscious and on the creative levels.

13. There are five general semantics tools which will assist you in creating a MetaBusiness ad. You may not specifically use them in the ad. Keeping them in mind, however, during the creative process will guide you out of the competitive level.

14. The five tools are: 1) Indexing, 2) Dating, 3) Etc., 4) Quotes, and 5) Hyphens.

15. What makes an advertisement a MetaBusiness ad? The quality of energy used to create the ad is of prime importance. Competitive advertising is based on fear. MetaBusiness advertising is based on the freedom to choose.

16. Next in importance are quality of words, images and sounds used in creating the MetaBusiness ads. All too often the words lowest, most, least, best, first, tallest, longest, shortest, complete, largest, etc. are overused and misused.

17. Another tendency of competitive advertising is to say too much in too small a space in display advertising, or too short a time in radio/TV advertising.

18. In MetaBusiness advertising you will often say and show less to communicate more. Remember, there are millions of people going through a transformation of consciousness. They can feel the energy quality of a MetaBusiness from their ad.

Chapter 12: MetaBusiness Connecting Planet Earth

Connecting Arizona

On May 1, 1990, I attended the *Connecting Arizona* party. *Connecting Arizona* is "The Natural Yellow Pages" for the State of Arizona. It is published annually by the Hampshire Group in Phoenix. The editor is Sara Riely.

I met Sara on April 12, 1990 at a friend's house in central Phoenix. We were gathered in a small group of three women and two men to tone with the accompaniment of a crystal bowl. Toning is a way of using the voice to raise your energy. After sharing this wonderful, high energy evening, Sara invited me to the *Connecting Arizona* party.

This gathering brought together the advertisers in "The Natural Yellow Pages". The categories included: Creative Arts and Entertainment, Counseling and Personal Growth, Food for Life, Holistic Healing, Business Services, Places to Grow and Know, Integrated Learning Therapies and Bodywork, Items for Enhancing Your Life and Spiritual and Intuitive Pathways.

Many of the people at the party were growing a MetaBusiness. They gathered together to support one another, to share information, to make new MetaBusiness contacts and to experience loving, creative, whole-living energies.

Sara writes in the preface of the 1990 edition of *Connecting Arizona*:

"My journey is about healing. I set out to find the people who live in their hearts and to make them my friends and my family. I have traveled from Sun City to Jerome, from Bisbee to Overgaard and everywhere I have been touched by those who have dared the darkness and now offer the best of who they are to those who come to seek their help.

"Angelic art, healing hands, places of stillness and beauty, books that help us soar, minerals and crystals and healing for body, mind and soul. Mine has been a joyous exploration."

Connecting Arizona is a MetaBusiness bringing together other MetaBusinesses. What Sara is doing along with her co-creators in Arizona is going on all over the world. MetaBusiness is in the process of Connecting Planet Earth.

What has happened in Arizona is a microcosm and a model for the future of a new global MetaBusiness community operating more on creative levels, not as much on a competitive levels. The *Connecting Arizona* party was an energizing experience, an uplifting experience and a non-competitive experience. As more states, regions, nations and groups of nations come together flying the earth flag on cooperative, creative levels, Connecting Planet Earth will become our daily experience. Perhaps May 1 will be celebrated around the world as Connecting Planet Earth Day.

Expos, Gatherings, Parties

Every year more MetaBusiness expos, gatherings and parties are created, giving a place and time to share MetaBusiness information, awareness and knowledge. Competitive businesses gather together at trade shows, conferences and service clubs to promote and sell their products and services.

MetaBusinesses gather to promote and sell on creative, cooperative, non-competitive levels. Also, their gatherings have a distinctly global feel. They do not restrict their consciousness into a limited city, state, regional, or national mind-set.

Since MetaBusinesses are not afraid of the competition, there is an openness, an acceptance, an embracing and a willingness to assist another growing MetaBusiness, even when it appears they are in the "same" business. Since one of the basic premises of a MetaBusiness is "There is a limitless supply in formless substance", being of service to a similar MetaBusiness can only nurture the growth of both businesses.

When MetaBusinesses gather Connecting Planet Earth, creative energies are released. Participants leave feeling energized, enriched, revitalized, enthused, and empowered. They feel numerous opportunities have come along effortlessly. The MetaBusiness purpose is renewed and the potential for more profits flows without competitive struggle or physically debilitating hard work.

The New Age Publishing And Retailing Alliance (NAPRA) is a MetaBusiness bringing together MetaBusinesses in expos, gatherings and parties. At the annual American Booksellers Association (ABA) convention they sponsor numerous events designed to inform, revitalize and connect. Some of the events for the 1990 ABA convention included the NAPRA networking gathering, NAPRA hospitality room, authors for a new decade breakfast, and Relaxation, Recovery and Music: The Common Ground of Sound.

NAPRA connects planet Earth by also representing its members at the Tokyo Book Fair and the Frankfurt Book Fair.

The Whole Life Expo is an annual gathering in San Francisco, Los Angeles, San Diego, and New York, which is described as "Three days of networking and fun". Their motto is "Healing Our Planet, Ourselves".

Hundreds of MetaBusinesses exhibit products/services which improve health and encourage personal growth, MetaBusinesses Connecting Planet Earth.

MetaBusiness Moving Mainstream

In January 1990, Stanford University Business School introduced a course, *New Paradigm Business*. Dr. Michael Ray teaches the course and describes it as follows:

"There is evidence that a paradigm shift (change in fundamental beliefs about the nature of the world) is occurring now in a scientific and therefore mundane sense that is equivalent of the Copernican Revolution of over four centuries ago. In business this has led to a shift from short-term financial goals to living our corporate and individual visions, from rigid to flexible cultures, from product to market orientation, from internal to external focus, from regional to global emphasis, from management direction to employees' self-management, from a procedural to a risk bias, from an analysis only approach to a creativity combination of both analysis and intuition, from a competition-only focus to that of cooperation, co-creation and contribution and from aggressive values to those of harmony, trust, honesty and compassion. The ultimate purpose of this New Paradigm Business is the enlightenment of those in it and the corresponding service to the community--to move beyond business through business."

"Beyond business - through business" is the motto of the World Business Academy.

"The World Business Academy provides a meeting ground where business leaders, entrepreneurs, practitioners and scholars can address the crucial role of business in shaping the global future. To this meeting ground business leaders bring their unique capabilities to convert vision into reality, and practitioners and scholars bring their skills of interpretation and analysis. It is this interaction which leads us beyond business through business."

The above quotes are from the World Business Academy brochure. John Renesch, World Business Academy member and director of Sterling and Stone, Inc., publishers of *The New Leaders* newsletter, wrote an article in the September 1989 World Business Academy newsletter, *Perspectives* titled *MetaBusiness: An Emergence of New Consciousness*. Renesch compares the attributes of emerging new business trends with those of a traditional competitive approaches.

To get a copy of John Renesch's article write or call the World Business Academy, 433 Airport Blvd., Suite 416, Burlingame, CA 94010 - 415-342-2387.

First Editions, a MetaBusiness focusing on connecting MetaBusinesses, recently proposed sponsoring an international conference with the theme "New Age Business: Moving Mainstream, Stepping Into the 1990s". The conference would focus on "moving material from the relatively limited conscious segment of the population to the broader and increasingly conscious general populace, both national and international."

MetaBusiness is indeed Moving Mainstream Connecting Planet Earth.

The MetaBusiness Card

A MetaBusiness card is different from a business card. A business card gives your name, address, telephone number and describes briefly what you do. A MetaBusiness card has another dimension. It carries a vibration, a feeling, an energy that gives a person the energetic quality of a business, a person, a product and a service.

True, a competitive business card also carries a vibration-feel. The difference is a competitive person does not consciously create the card; they unconsciously put together the card. Their concern is more with image, impression, title and negative ego.

The MetaBusiness person is not interested in these superficial, infantile concerns. They want their MetaBusiness card to be a vibrational calling card. When someone picks up their MetaBusiness card, they want them to get a feeling. Some of the feelings may include: trust, quality, love, service, peace, choice, etc.

It is wise for a MetaBusiness person to take a lot of care, time and attention in creating their MetaBusiness card. Going to a printer and slapping one together in a mad rush is not advisable. The rush frequency, which can be quite irritating, will be loaded into the card.

Card stock color, card stock texture, ink colors, logo design, type styles, layout, lettering size, wording, etc., combine to create a feeling given by your MetaBusiness. Often people hold on to a MetaBusiness card for months and years. A heartfelt, distinct look and feel will increase the quality-vibration made on the consciousness of a present and potential customer.

On one of my book promotion trips I visited a MetaBusiness and complimented the owner on her MetaBusiness card. I told her that she obviously spent a lot of care, time and attention creating her card. She thanked me and then asked how I could tell the difference from a traditional competitive business card. I told her the card had an energy which emanated feelings of quality, care, love, trust, honesty, sensitivity, consciousness and creativity.

You might take a tip from this successful MetaBusiness woman. She collected dozens of MetaBusiness cards. She then laid them out on a table and looked them over allowing her attention to focus in on specific cards and specific aspects of cards which she liked.

Next, she wrote down what attracted her eye: cardstock, colors, typestyles, layouts, etc. It became clear to her how she wanted her MetaBusiness card to look. See if you can notice the difference between a MetaBusiness card and a competitive business card. Review your business card. Next time you print it you may want to make some creative changes.

Getting Down To MetaBusiness

There is an evolutionary force activating a global change in consciousness. Individuals by the millions are experiencing personal transformations. As a result our cultural institutions are changing at an accelerated rate.

Look at health care, political systems, science, education, entertainment, communications, family, religion, etc. The institutions and systems of the 1950s and 1960s are radically different in the 1990s. The business and economic institutions and systems are in the midst of an evolutionary transformation away from a competitive, fear-based system into a creative, consciousness-oriented system.

As business leaders become MetaBusiness leaders their conscious decisions to "go with the flow" of evolutionary change will accelerate and stabilize the changes going on in all the other cultural areas. "Money talks." When MetaBusiness cash flow is invested on a creative level, institutions are visibly and functionally transformed in a relatively short time.

Business practices pervade every life area from family to spiritual. By getting down to MetaBusiness and getting off the competitive levels, the evolutionary process of connecting planet earth on creative levels will be crystallized.

Getting down to MetaBusiness means:

1. Balancing purpose and profit
2. Staying on the creative levels
3. Being grateful
4. Whole living
5. Living rhythmically
6. Balancing intuition and intellect
7. Focusing on the limitless supply

These seven skills are more than intellectual ideas that sound good. To be on the creative level requires functional ability. Excitement and enthusiasm about creating a MetaBusiness is not the living, active, everyday practice of the above skills.

In most instances it requires steady, long-term effort to gradually let go of competitive habits and persistently and flexibly function on the creative MetaBusiness levels. Please do not identify the idea level with the functional level. You're better off staying on the competitive level and knowing it than thinking you're on the creative level but functioning on the competitive level.

A Global Race Psyche

Have you gone to a Wendy's or Sizzler restaurant lately? Look at the all-you-can-eat salad bar. Pastas, tacos, three-bean salad, tuna salad, etc. The salad bar is going global, international, whole earth.

At one meal we are eating foods that are traditionally from Mexico, Italy, France, Germany, Japan, England, Denmark, Greece, etc. Our tastebuds and stomachs are global. MetaBusiness is connecting planet earth into a global race psyche.

A global economic, social, political and spiritual cross-pollination process is unfolding before our very eyes. Jet planes, technological bumblebees, take off and land from cultural flowers. A new honey is now being created with a flavor that will satisfy the tastebuds of people around the world.

The language of business, both the competitive and the MetaBusiness, is English. When I met with my Singapore printer in Las Vegas, Nevada, our meeting was in English. When I met with my foreign rights agent in Sausalito, California (who is originally from Germany), our meeting was in English.

The organic process away from national race psyches to a global race psyche is accelerating in the 1990s at "breakneck speed". MetaBusinesses and specifically MetaBusiness co-creators are functionally the most capable in assisting the evolutionary forces.

Being conscious and aware in the moment, they are less resistant to change. Being grateful and appreciative, they are less greedy. Being more in tune with their purpose, they are, therefore, more in tune with the purpose-of-the-whole.

On a practical everyday level MetaBusinesses are connecting planet earth in a global race psyche because they rent an office and spend money to make money. AT&T now has international 800 phone service to over 50 countries. UPS has service to 175 countries and territories. The Wall Street Journal can publish editions in different parts of the world on the same day via satellite.

In order for the global race psyche to form properly and survive its infancy, we must ground ourselves on the creative levels and continually release and let go more and more of the fearful, greedy, competitive levels.

Summary of Chapter 12

1. *Connecting Arizona* is a MetaBusiness bringing together other MetaBusinesses. What Sara is doing along with her co-creators in Arizona is going on all over the world.

2. As more states, regions, nations and groups of nations come together flying the earth flag on cooperative, creative levels, Connecting Planet Earth will become our daily experience.

3. Every year more MetaBusiness expos, gatherings and parties are created giving a place and time to share MetaBusiness information, awareness, and knowledge.

4. When MetaBusinesses gather Connecting Planet Earth, a "high energy" is released. Participants leave feeling energized, enriched, revitalized, enthused and empowered.

5. They feel numerous opportunities have come along effortlessly. The MetaBusiness purpose is renewed and the potential for more profits follows without competitive struggle or physically debilitating hard work.

6. "Beyond business - through business" is the motto of the World Business Academy. "The World Business Academy provides a meeting ground where business leaders, entrepreneurs, practitioners and scholars can address the crucial role of business in shaping the global future."

7. A MetaBusiness card carries a vibration, a feeling, an energy that tells a person the energetic quality of a business, a person, a product and a service.

8. Some of the feelings a MetaBusiness card may carry include: trust, quality, love, service, peace, choice, etc.

9. The business and economic institutions and systems are in the midst of an evolutionary transformation away from a competitive, fear-based system into a creative, consciousness-oriented system.

10. Business practices pervade every life area from family to spiritual. By getting down to MetaBusiness and getting off the competitive levels - the evolutionary process of connecting planet earth on creative levels will be crystallized.

11. Getting down to MetaBusiness means: 1) balancing purpose and profit, 2) staying on the creative levels, 3) being grateful, 4) whole living, 5) living rhythmically, 6) balancing intuition and intellect, and 7) focusing on the limitless supply.

12. In most instances it requires steady, long-term effort to gradually let go of competitive habits and persistently and flexibly function on the creative MetaBusiness levels.

13. At one meal we are eating foods that are traditionally from Mexico, Italy, France, Germany, Japan, England, Denmark, Greece, etc. Our tastebuds and stomachs are global. MetaBusiness is connecting planet earth into a global race psyche.

14. Jet planes, technological bumblebees, take off and land from cultural flowers. A new honey (manna from heaven) is now being created with a flavor that will satisfy the tastebuds of people around the world.

15. The organic process away from national race psyches to a global race psyche is accelerating in the 1990s at "breakneck speed". MetaBusinesses and specifically MetaBusiness co-creators are functionally the most capable in assisting the evolutionary forces.

16. In order for the global race psyche to form properly and survive its infancy, we must ground ourselves on the creative levels and continually release and let go more and more of the fearful, greedy, competitive levels.

Chapter 13: MetaBusiness Transforming Your Life

Self-Remembering and Self-Observation

A MetaBusiness that is firmly yet flexibly connected with the creative levels becomes an environment for transforming your life. It is not just work place where you put in your time and use up your energy. A MetaBusiness encourages you to transform your life by transmuting energy.

Besides having a men's room and a women's room, a MetaBusiness has an Energy Room. An Energy Room is a place you can go to rejuvenate your energies when you are feeling tired, drained, stuck, unfocused, tense, hyper, upset, nervous, fearful, confused, blocked, depressed, angry, etc.

The meaning of the words "I have to go" will include the Energy Room. It will be just as acceptable to go to the Energy Room as it is to go to the men's room or women's room. No one will think twice about it. When your energies are "off", it makes sense to realign your energies. The quality of your co-creative work/play will be immediately enhanced.

In order, however, for a MetaBusiness to be a place for transforming your life, it presupposes self-remembering and self-observation. Simply stated, you must be aware. Awareness means, first, the decision to self-remember, and, second, actually self-remembering regularly and rhythmically.

To self-remember try this. Say to yourself attentively "I (say your name) am completely aware in the here-now". Say it three times in a row with attentiveness. Do this many times a day especially when you first wake up.

Self-remembering leads naturally into self-observation. Turn your awareness on yourself. Notice without judgement. Forget "right/wrong", "good/bad". Just notice. There's no need to analyze. No need to criticize. Observe your thoughts, feelings, emotions, tensions, likes, dislikes, actions, and reactions.

Observe your energy level continuously. Do you feel energized? Do you feel energetically balanced and centered? Do you feel hyper? Are you rushing? Are you tired or drained?

Knowing through self-remembering and self-observation that your energies are off, you then take action to balance and center, transforming your energies and your life.

Physical Repose

One of the master keys to transforming your life is physical repose. Observe the tensions in your body. Focus your attention in the back of your neck. What do you feel? Are you tense? Are you relaxed? Can you feel the difference?

Staying on the creative levels requires physical repose. Physical repose is a state of focused relaxation, of attention without tension. Physical repose results from a process of letting go of habitual and mechanical postures.

There are four basic body positions. From least active to most active they are:

1. Lying Down

2. Sitting

3. Standing

4. Walking

By observing yourself several times a day in each of the four basic body positions, notice where you hold tension. Focus your attention in different parts of your body and feel the tension.

Once you feel a tense area, gradually bring your attention into the center of the tension. There's a tendency for the tension to repel attention. Return rhythmically and gently with your attention into the tension.

Next time you notice excess tension, lie down on the floor. You can do this in your office or perhaps in the Energy Room or at home. Now give your weight up to the floor. Do you notice how you hold onto yourself. Let the floor hold you up. Give your body up to the floor. It is certainly strong enough to hold you up. Experience physical repose.

When sitting anywhere, at your desk, in your car, in a waiting room, etc., give your body up to the chair. Go into physical repose by letting go. Allow the chair to do the work of holding you up.

Physical repose while standing is an excellent way to transmute energies. Put your attention in your feet. Feel the soles of your feet touching the floor or ground. Let the floor/ground/earth support you. Give your weight up, let go. Attention without tension. Focused relaxation. Physical repose.

Observe your body next time you walk. Do you hold yourself in the shoulders, neck, back, hips, etc.? Be more fluid and flexible. Release the tensions. Walk in physical repose.

Physical repose provides a reservoir of life energy to draw on. You will be continually regenerating your energies as you go about your MetaBusiness.

Emotional Calm

To maintain a continuous connection to the creative levels, you must practice emotional calm. Practicing emotional calm is a skill that can be learned. Once learned you will be free of the competitive levels.

Let me describe to you an actual incident which demonstrates what I mean by emotional calm. I finished a business meeting in downtown San Francisco about 3 pm. I went to the parking garage, got in my car and drove off.

I was feeling in a hurry (remember Chapter 6: Rhythm Replaces Rush). I wanted to get out of the city before "rush" hour. I turned down a main street heading for an interstate. I got stuck in a traffic jam due to construction.

As the minutes went by, I became more and more upset. I moved one block in ten minutes. I was angry. I imagined I'd be stuck there for hours. Emotionally I was becoming unglued.

Here was an opportunity for me to practice emotional calm and get off the competitive rush frequency. By the way, most everyone in the cars around me was in an emotional turmoil as well. That traffic jam created quite an emotional vortex. Can you identify with my experience?

How to practice emotional calm?

Step 1 Observe Your Emotional State.

> Notice everything you can about your emotional reaction. I felt the anger in my stomach. Negative thoughts raced through my mind. My body tensed up. My breathing was shallow.

Step 2 Choose Not To Identify.

> Once you become conscious of your emotional state, you have the freedom to choose not to identify. Once I realized I was tuning into the anger frequency, I chose not to tune into it any longer.

Step 3 Breathe Rhythmically.

> Inhale gently through the nose; exhale slowly through the nose. Keep it up for a minute or two. As I breathed rhythmically in the midst of that traffic jam, I felt the emotional grip begin to let go.

Step 4 Self-Remember.

> Say to yourself "I (*your name*) am completely aware in the here-now." Look and listen in total awareness.

As I did that my awareness turned to a side street on my right. I felt intuitively to take that street even though it was not in the direction I wanted to go. I turned down that street. It was a clear shot for six blocks, running into the street I needed to take me to the interstate.

Peace of Mind

Staying on the creative levels and off the competitive levels is achieved more easily by practicing "peace of mind". What is "peace of mind"? Peace of mind is a state of mental repose where the steady stream of thoughts, words and images moving through the mental field is not **unconsciously** identified with.

While going through your day, whether at work, at home or out and about, self-remember. Become acutely aware in the moment. Observe the thoughts, words and images passing through your mind.

Just observe. Notice. Set aside all your judgments about good or bad, right or wrong. Simply observe. Set aside analysis and figuring out for another time. As you allow thoughts, words and images to flow into the mind, stay in the mind and leave the mind, you steady the mind. The mental field becomes more peaceful and quiet. The Buddha spoke of peace of mind as follows:

Like an archer an arrow,
the wise man steadies his trembling mind,
A fickle and restless weapon.
Flapping like a fish thrown on dry ground,
it trembles all day, struggling
to escape from the snares of ignorance.
The mind is restless.
to control it is sane.
A disciplined mind is the road to true freedom.
Swift, single, nebulous
it sits in the cave of the heart
who conquers it, frees himself from the slavery of ignorance.
No point calling him wise
whose mind is unsteady
who is not calm
who does not know the way.
Call him wise
whose mind is calm,
whose senses are controlled,
who is unaffected by positive and negative
who is aware.

In order to achieve greater peace of mind review how to stop automatic thinking on page 7-6 and 7-7. The five steps are:

1. Become Aware

2. Breath Rhythmically

3. Activate the Five Senses

4. Become Body Conscious

5. Relax.

The Spiritual Frequencies

A MetaBusiness environment is a spiritual environment. Physical repose, emotional calm and peace of mind create a space for spiritual frequencies like love, joy, play, understanding, will, humor, creativity, spontaneity, compassion, wisdom, etc., to thrive. These life-enriching qualities have a rate of vibration, cycles per unit of time. They can be felt and experienced when your consciousness is tuned to their specific frequency.

It's about time we bring heartfelt, energizing spirituality into our workday. This process is happening around the world. Inwardly, quietly and without pretense people are attuning themselves to the spiritual frequencies during the workday. Visualization, meditation, rhythmic breathing, relaxation, etc., are being used to rejuvenate, regenerate, renew and realign.

Competitive business environments do not, for the most part, encourage or accept revitalizing practices. It is considered unproductive and a "waste of time". Do it on your own time if you must but not on company time. Yet millions are silently and invisibly tuning to the spiritual frequencies, a few moments here and there in the midst of the fearful competitive levels.

People tell me everywhere I travel they take bathroom breaks in order to visualize, relax, meditate, breath rhythmically and tune into the spiritual frequencies of love, light and wisdom. If competitive leaders knew what these creative workers were doing, they probably would not like it. Yet they reap the benefits. A relaxed, calm and peaceful individual tends to be more alert, efficient, sensitive to changing conditions, productive and creative.

MetaBusiness leaders and caretakers are looking for and hiring people who make whole living, balanced living and attunement to the spiritual frequencies an integral part of their life. A MetaBusiness openly encourages their co-creators to rhythmically alternate from activity to rest whenever needed.

Waiting to get home after work or until the weekend to tune into the spiritual frequencies and realign your energies is usually too long to wait. The imbalance often becomes greater. Usually it is better to do something about tensions, emotional disturbances and excessive thinking as soon as possible.

With an open, accepting and encouraging approach of a MetaBusiness, balance is restored more quickly. The quality of work stays on a creative level. The spiritual frequencies thrive.

Renewing Your Purpose

There are times when it is wise to renew your purpose. Perhaps things are not going as smoothly. Maybe several difficulties arise one after the other. You may feel overwhelmed, frustrated, discouraged, etc. Feelings of lack may grip you.

A MetaBusiness environment allows and encourages the transformation of your life. Remember, when you are in a down cycle to take time to renew your purpose. Purpose is at the heart of a MetaBusiness. An unwavering purpose anchors you to the creative levels and keeps you off the competitive levels.

What can you do to renew your purpose?

Step 1 Hold your attention steady on the limitless supply in formless substance.

Notice the leaves on the trees. How many leaves are there on a tree? On all the trees on the earth? On all the earth-like planets in all the universe?

Notice the stars at night. How many stars are there in all the universe? As you continue holding your attention on the limitless supply in formless substance, you will notice your feelings of lack will begin to fall away.

You will begin to feel expansive, full of faith that things will work out and confident that new possibilities and opportunities are right around the corner.

Step 2   Maintain a deep, continuous and devout feeling of gratitude.

Whatever you look at, whatever you touch, be grateful. Appreciate all the wonderful and even the not-so-wonderful experiences and people in your life. Know that whatever happens is a necessary lesson, part of a learning process. Be grateful. Give thanks. Heartfelt feelings of gratitude will energize your purpose.

Step 3   Refocus your vision.

In your mind's-eye see what it is you want to create. See it clearly. Perhaps new aspects of your original vision will emerge. This refocusing process will give your purpose new clarity. Fuzzy vision often leads to chaotic, confused and mixed manifestations in products, services, customer relations, cash flow, employer/employee co-creator interactions.

Step 4   Ask for guidance.

Whatever you call the universal mind, the higher power, the force, God, the eternal, etc., makes little difference. Ask for guidance in whatever way makes you comfortable. Whether it is prayer, meditation, silence... ask for guidance.

To receive assistance, you must ask. This is the law of free will. Intervention or "help" without permission is not permitted. To do so without permission is a violation of an individual's "divine rights". Ask with deep sincerity and always with a willingness to do your part.

Summary of Chapter 13

1. A MetaBusiness that is firmly yet flexibly connected with the creative levels becomes an environment for transforming your life.

2. An Energy Room is a place you can go to rejuvenate your energies when you are feeling tired, drained, stuck, unfocused, tense, hyper, upset, nervous, fearful, confused, blocked, depressed, angry, etc.

3. In order for a MetaBusiness to be a place for transforming your life, it presupposes self-remembering and self-observation.

4. Knowing through self-remembering and self-observation that your energies are off, you then take action to balance and center, transforming your energies and your life.

5. Staying on the creative levels requires physical repose. Physical repose is a state of focused relaxation, of attention without tension. Physical repose results from a process of letting go of habitual and mechanical postures.

6. Once you feel a tense area, gradually bring your attention into the center of the tension. There's a tendency for the tension to repel attention. Return rhythmically and gently with your attention into the tension.

7. Physical repose provides a reservoir of life energy to draw on. You will be continuously regenerating your energies as you go about your MetaBusiness.

8. To maintain a continuous connection to the creative levels, you must practice emotional calm.

9. How to practice emotional calm: 1) Observe Your Emotional State, 2) Choose Not To Identify, 3) Breathe Rhythmically, and 4) Self-Remember.

10. Staying on the creative levels and off the competitive levels is achieved more easily by practicing "peace of mind".

11. Peace of mind is a state of mental repose where the steady stream of thoughts, words and images moving through the mental field is not unconsciously identified with.

12. As you allow thoughts, words and images to flow into the mind, stay in the mind and leave the mind, you steady the mind. The mental field becomes more peaceful and quiet.

13. Physical repose, emotional calm and peace of mind create a space for spiritual frequencies like love, joy, play, understanding, will, humor, creativity, spontaneity, compassion, wisdom, etc., to thrive.

14. Inwardly, quietly and without pretense, people are attuning themselves to the spiritual frequencies during the workday. Visualization, meditation, rhythmic breathing, and relaxation are being used to rejuvenate, regenerate, renew and realign.

15. MetaBusiness leaders and caretakers are looking for and hiring people who make whole living, balanced living and attunement to the spiritual frequencies an integral part of their life.

16. A MetaBusiness openly encourages their co-creators to rhythmically alternate from activity to rest whenever needed.

17. Remember, when you are in a down cycle to take time to renew your purpose. Purpose is at the heart of a MetaBusiness. An unwavering purpose anchors you to the creative levels and keeps you off the competitive levels.

18. What can you do to renew your purpose? 1) Hold your attention steady on the limitless supply in formless substance, 2) Maintain a deep, continuous and devout feeling of gratitude, 3) Refocus your vision, 4) Ask for guidance.

About the Energy Room

We can design and create an Energy Room for your business, company, or corporation. We will train your co-creator employees how to use the Energy Room to maintain a productive energy level. Call the MetaBusiness Institute at 1-800-322-9943.

About the Author

Greg Nielsen is an internationally known author and lecturer. His books have been translated into several languages including German, Japanese, and Spanish. He has more than twenty years experience in the "consciousness movement" beginning with extensive training under the guidance of Joseph Campbell's protege, Francoise Nesbitte. His main focus is assisting others in the process of integrating awareness of energies in the work-a-day world.

About the Artist

Joanne Dose received her training in commercial and fine art at the Art Institute of Chicago and the University of Wisconsin at Madison. An accomplished visionary artist, Joanne has designed numerous covers, including Greg Nielsen's book *Tuning to the Spiritual Frequencies*. A national following of private collectors display her higher self and light being portraits in their homes and offices.

Note

To order the book *Scientific Financial Success* and the MetaBusiness audio cassettes, write:

Conscious Books
316 California Avenue, Suite 210
Reno, Nevada 89509

Join the
MetaBusiness Institute

Annual Membership: $99

You will receive the following:

- Our monthly newsletter, MetaBusiness Journal
- 20% discount on weekly classes
- 10% discount on consultations (in person or over the telephone), correspondence courses, books and tapes, Institute-sponsored seminars and more!

Make your check for $99.00 payable to the MetaBusiness Institute and mail to:

**MetaBusiness Institute
316 California Avenue, Suite 210
Reno, Nevada 89509**

For a free newsletter and to find out about the next MetaBusiness Institute seminar, **Energy . . . Transforming Your Life,** call 800/322-9943.

Greg Nielsen, Michelle Schmidt, and other faculty members of the MetaBusiness Institute conduct seminars and "Funshops" for corporate clients as well as the general public. For more information on sponsoring a seminar or "Funshop" in your city or at your place of business, contact the Institute at 800/322-9943.